Case Studies in the Developing World

7

Tourism and Development in Africa

W. P. Gamble

Senior Lecturer in Geography and Head of Afro-Asian Studies
Edge Hill College of Higher Education, Ormskirk

John Murray

Case Studies in the Developed World

General Editors   Hilary Winchester and David Pickard

Agricultural Change: France and the EEC   Hilary Winchester and Brian Ilbery

Industrial Change: New England and Appalachia   Michael Bradshaw

Shops and Offices: Locational Change in Britain and the EEC   Michael Bateman

Population Change: the American South   Robert Estall

Case Studies in the Developing World

General Editors   Robert W. Bradnock and Robin Holmes

Agricultural Change in South Asia   Robert W. Bradnock

Urbanisation in India   Robert W. Bradnock

Population and Development in Peru   Clifford T. Smith

Transport and Development in Tropical Africa   Brian Hoyle

Oil and Development in the Gulf   Keith and Anne McLachlan

Agricultural Change in Nigeria   Kathleen M. Baker

Tourism and Development in Africa   W. P. Gamble

© W. P. Gamble 1989

First published 1989
by John Murray (Publishers) Ltd
50 Albemarle Street
London W1X 4BD

Typeset by Pioneer, Associates, Perthshire
Printed and bound in Great Britain by
Butler & Tanner Ltd, Frome and London

British Library Cataloguing in Publication Data

Gamble, W. P.
  Tourism and development in Africa.
  (Case studies in the developing world).
  1. Africa. economic conditions. Effects
of tourism
  I. Title   II. series
  338.4'7916

ISBN 0-7195-4496-3

Contents

Acknowledgements

I am very grateful to Norah Ball, Ann Chapman and Jane Pugh for drawing the figures. I also very much appreciate the constructive advice and assistance of Bob Bradnock, Robin Holmes and Roger Millman and the patience and support from the staff at John Murray who supervised the preparation of the book. A small research grant from Edge Hill College of Higher Education made it possible to visit Tunisia, and use productively the libraries of the School of Oriental and African Studies, London University and the Hollins Annex, Manchester Polytechnic. Statistics related to the five case-studies were directly obtained from the Egyptian National Tourist Office, London; the Ministry of Economic Planning and Industrial Development, Banjul, The Gambia; the Ministry of Tourism and Wildlife, Nairobi, Kenya; the Statistics Division, President's Office, Victoria, The Seychelles; and the Tunisian National Tourist Offices in Sousse, Tunisia and London. I am particularly grateful to Mr Ghozzi, the Director of the Tunisian National Tourist Office in London who was most helpful and encouraging.

Figure 5 was adapted from a diagram originally appearing on page 91 in P. E. Murphy, *Tourism, a Community Approach* published by Methuen and Co. in 1985. Figure 6 first appeared on page 277 in M. Barke, and G. O'Hare, *The Third World* published by Oliver and Boyd in 1985. Figure 22 was adapted from a diagram which first appeared in an article by Stanley C. Plog in *The Cornell Hotel and Restaurant Administration Quarterly*, February 1974.

Photographs are reproduced courtesy of: Barnaby's Picture Library (page 46); G Cubitt (Barnaby's Picture Library) (page 39); Robin Holmes (page 34); Hubertus Kanus (Barnaby's Picture Library) (page 30); Ken Lambert (Barnaby's Picture Library) (page 29); Mavis Ronson (Barnaby's Picture Library) (page 26); the Tunisian Tourist Board (pages 14, 16 and 25).

Examination questions have been reproduced by permission of the following examination boards: the Associated Examining Board, the Joint Matriculation Board, the Oxford and Cambridge Schools Examination Board and the University of London Schools Examination Board.

Sources of statistics

The Economist Intelligence Reports.
EGAPT (Egyptian General Authority for the Promotion of Tourism), *Tourist Statistics Information 1980-4.*
The Gambia: Central Statistical Department, Ministry of Economic Planning and Industrial Development, *Tourism Statistics 1984-5.*
HMSO, *Social Trends, 1985.*
Kenya: Ministry of Planning and National Development, *Economic Survey 1986.*
The Seychelles: Statistical Division, *Migration and Tourism Statistics 1985.*
Tunisia: Organisation National de la Tourisme Tunisienne, *Evolution de l'Industrie Touristique* (1986).
United Nations, 'World Statistics in Brief' from *The Statistical Yearbook* (9th edition).
World Bank, *World Development Report 1985.*
World Tourist Organisation, *World Travel and Tourism Statistics, 1982-3.*
World Travel News 1979.

I would also like to thank my wife Jean and my family for putting up with my efforts at writing, and dedicate this book to them.

W.P.G.

Introduction

Over the last few years African countries have been invaded not by armies but by pleasure seekers. These recent invaders come mainly from Europe. They are part of the ever-increasing flow of international tourists. Generally, they are welcomed by the host African governments since they spend money. They transfer money earned in rich countries to poor African countries. Many of these poor countries see tourists as providing money which will encourage economic development.

International tourism has a significant impact, economically, socially and spatially, on the more popular African destinations. Not only is more money brought into the country but opportunities and tensions are created through contact between the tourists and local people.

Attracting tourists to distant lands is expensive. Although tourist attractions (the **resources**) such as sun, sand, sea, natural fauna, monuments and traditions may be 'free', they have to be reached, which means building airports and roads (the **infrastructure**) and the tourists have to be made comfortable and entertained in hotels and restaurants (the **superstructure**). It is also necessary to plan the resorts, to advertise overseas, to train workers in new skills and to set up travel agencies. Much money is required even before the first tourist arrives. This can be provided by the government, by local business people or can come from abroad. This money will not then be available for other projects, so the decision to invest in tourism must be justified. Invariably, the justification, especially by official bodies, is that international tourism contributes to development. This book examines this claim in detail.

The recent rapid growth in international tourism is of considerable interest to the geographer. According to Professor D. M. Smith, geography is concerned with who gets what, where and how. The study of international tourism looks at the movement of people, money and goods, the impact tourism has and the means by which it takes place. Neither the movement of people nor the impact of tourism is uniform. Some African countries have attracted large numbers of tourists while others have not. In the former, the familiar tourist landscape of resorts now exists, while, in the latter, such resorts are largely absent. This is a further element of difference between countries which geographers seek to explain. Such explanations need to go beyond an assessment of tourist attractions. Why, for instance, has Tunisia managed to attract large numbers of sun-seeking tourists while neighbouring Algeria and Libya, which have similar climate and beaches, have failed to do so? The answer lies in political and social differences which determine attitudes and priorities.

This book opens with two chapters which look at the recent growth of international tourism in Africa. Chapter 1 explores the economic and social reasons why an increasing number of people from developed countries are not only travelling abroad for their holidays but visiting developing regions such as Africa. Chapter 2 considers why many African governments are trying to attract international tourists. The final two chapters focus on the experience of five contrasting African countries, all of which have developed a tourist industry, and assess the economic, social and spatial impact of tourism.

1
International tourism since 1951

'Travel will do you good by giving you knowledge of people, shapes of mountains, plains extending to unknown lengths, valleys with eternal waters trickling through [but] you will not become better or more sensible.' (Seneca, Roman philosopher and playwright, 4BC—55AD)

The growth of international tourism

International tourism has become one of the world's largest and most rapidly expanding economic activities. Table 1 shows how international tourism has increased since 1951. As an earner of foreign exchange, it is becoming increasingly important when compared with other exports. In 1951, earnings from tourism were 3.4% of the total global export earnings. In 1984, this proportion had risen to 5.1%. Even during the world recession from 1980 to 1983, earnings from tourism still grew although there was an 11% decline in the value of exported goods. Tourism has now become an important and dynamic sector of the economy in many countries.

The figures in Table 1 exclude tourists who do not leave their home country (domestic tourists) and excursionists who stay in a foreign country for less than 24 hours. This book focuses on **international tourists**: people who, mainly in pursuit of pleasure, cross a frontier and stay for at least 24 hours in a foreign country. In so doing they spend money earned in one country in another and thereby contribute to the international flow of resources.

Reasons for growth

For many people today the urge to travel can readily be satisfied. About 80% of international tourists come from the rich industrial economies of North America, Western Europe, Japan and Australasia. In these regions, since 1951, many people have had the advantage of higher incomes, more leisure and cheaper transport. Also there has been the development of the 'package' holiday, which has made it easy to make journeys to almost anywhere in the world.

Table 1   International tourism since 1951

Year	Numbers (millions)	Receipts ($US billions)
1951	25	2.0
1961	75	7.3
1965	116	11.8
1970	168	17.9
1971	172	20.9
1972	182	24.8
1973	191	31.2
1974	198	34.1
1975	215	38.6
1976	221	44.9
1977	234	54.4
1978	258	68.7
1979	270	82.2
1980	279	95.3
1981	284	96.0
1982	288	94.6
1983	294	96.2
1984	312	101.0
1985	325	105.0

A look at the history of exploration and travel clearly illustrates people's desire to visit strange places and seek new experiences. This impulse may well have been strengthened by the pressures of living in urbanised, industrial countries. The rest, relaxation and change which foreign travel offers, are now considered by many almost as basic needs. A French newspaper survey in the early 1970s revealed that many French people preferred to save money on motoring and food rather than on holidays. This seems typical of people living in rich countries. A holiday has become a regular annual event, not to be missed at any cost.

Motives for travel

The motives for travel can be considered under four headings: psychological, cultural, social and escapist. Most people periodically feel that they need a change.

If they go away, rest and relax they know they will feel better for it. This is the psychological motive. In a sample survey of American travellers published in 1980, 63% of those interviewed mentioned 'rest and relaxation' as one of the main reasons for travel, while 50% cited 'escape from routine'. The survey noted a shift of attitude within the United States from the work ethic to a search for 'a more complete way of life'. Travel and tourism played an important part in this search.

Cultural reasons for travel include improving the mind and expanding knowledge. There was a leisured class of Romans who had the time and means to travel for pleasure. Such a class did not emerge again in the western world until late mediaeval Europe, when groups began to visit the Holy Land via Venice. Subsequently, the 'Grand Tour', which aimed at completing the education of the British aristocracy, became fashionable. A tutor invariably accompanied the young noble on the 'Grand Tour'. Today an enthusiasm for history, culture and scholarship, as well as nostalgia, are important motives for travel. University lecturers are employed to accompany special interest tours to places of historic, cultural or natural interest. Ancient monuments have been preserved and restored to attract tourists.

Within rich, industrial societies, travel has become more or less a social necessity. It is no longer a sign of exceptional wealth and leisure as was the 'Grand Tour' but is an expected yearly ritual for all. For some people the main aim of this ritual is a sun tan. Since the emergence of the Côte d'Azur in southern France as a summer resort in the 1930s, 'horizontal holidays', consisting mainly of lying on a beach in the sun in order to get a tan, have grown rapidly in popularity. Far more people now go on these 'sunlust' holidays than on special interest tours ('wanderlust' holidays). Resorts have grown up, particularly in Caribbean and Mediterranean countries, to cater for the sunlust holidaymaker.

Escapism underpins the three motives so far discussed. International travel companies exploit the desire of many people to escape to a place where the sun always shines and life is carefree and uncomplicated. The island of Jerba, one of Tunisia's main holiday resorts, is promoted as Ulysses' island of the lotus eaters, where people lived in a dream-like state. Those who ate the lotus were supposed to lose all thoughts of home. At the resorts, the illusion of simplicity, warmth and 'traditional' values is encouraged by the staging of 'pseudo-events': entertainments based loosely on folklore and tradition but adapted for tourists. Thus, in Tunisia, a tourist can experience a 'Bedouin Feast', as well as a 'traditional' wedding. One company, Club Méditerranée, has based its very successful marketing policy on escapism. The aim of its holiday villages is 'to give back to urban vacationers the village of old with all its freedoms'. For most people holidays should be an opportunity for carefree relaxation in a cosy environment.

Opportunities for travel

Many people who live in the developed countries now have the leisure and means to travel. Leisure is defined as the time available after sleep, eating and work. In the main tourist source regions leisure has increased in three ways: a shorter working week, longer paid holidays and earlier retirement. The shortening of the working week is of little relevance to international tourism. However, the general increase in the length of paid holidays is significant. The 1938 Holidays with Pay Act in Britain meant that, at the end of the Second World War, 14 million people received pay while on holiday. The length of paid holidays has

Table 2   Length of paid holidays in Britain, 1963–84

	Length of paid holidays (% of total)						
Year	Up to 2 weeks	2–3 weeks	3 weeks	3–4 weeks	4 weeks	4–5 weeks	Over 5 weeks
1963	96	2	2	—	—	—	—
1966	63	34	3	—	—	—	—
1969	51	35	10	1	—	—	—
1972	10	14	60	16	2	—	—
1975	1	1	18	50	30	—	—
1978	—	1	18	46	35	—	—
1981	—	—	2	15	23	59	1
1984	—	—	—	6	13	60	20

increased rapidly over the last 20 years, as shown in Table 2.

Three factors have contributed to the growing demand for long stay, out of season holidays recently. First, the age of retirement has been progressively lowered. Secondly, more people are choosing early retirement. Thirdly, a growing proportion of people in developed countries are reaching retirement age while still fit and healthy.

Since 1951, wages have risen more rapidly than the cost of living. The average person in work has more money left over after paying for food, housing, fuel, light and taxes. Over the last 15 years, the average British worker has become £40 to £50 a week better off in the equivalent of 1984 prices. Some of this extra money has been spent on overseas travel (see Table 3).

The number of people from the UK taking holidays abroad doubled between 1971 and 1983. No doubt more leisure and money contributed to this but two other factors had an influence: the decline in the real cost of medium- and long-haul public transport and the growing popularity of the all inclusive 'package' holiday. The first point is illustrated by Table 4, which shows the improvement in both speed and real cost of travelling between New York and other cities. These improvements are partly due to changes in technology. After 1945, aircraft rapidly replaced ocean liners as the main form of intercontinental travel. The introduction of jet aircraft in the late 1950s doubled the speed of air travel and the wide-bodied jets of the 1970s reduced the average cost per person (unit cost). Consequently, more and more people living in developed countries were able to consider holidays in distant lands. The Caribbean can now be reached easily by people from America and Canada and the Mediterranean by people from north west Europe. More and more Japanese and Australian people are

Table 3   Destination of UK holidaymakers

Year	Destination in UK (millions of people)	Overseas (millions of people)
1951	25.00	1.50
1961	31.50	3.50
1971	34.00	7.00
1976	38.00	7.00
1983	34.00	15.00
1984	34.00	16.00

visiting the countries of the South China Sea. These have become the sunbelt destinations of tourists from rich, industrial countries. The more prosperous and adventurous are travelling even further, so that much of the Third World is now part of the international tourist periphery.

The growth of the 'package' holiday has made it much easier for people to go abroad. Specialist companies arrange travel to the country, accommodation, meals, transfers from the destination airport to the hotel, insurance and even entertainment and tours within the country visited (see Figure 1, p. 4). The tourist pays one basic price, though there may be optional extras for tours and entertainment. This saves the tourist time and also money, for the travel company can negotiate cheaper aircraft and hotel prices. Besides, travelling in groups is comforting for the inexperienced and uncertain tourist. The group forms its own protecting and familiar society. From this secure haven the tourist can observe and discuss with like-minded people the features and way of life of the host country.

Travellers may be classified as drifters, explorers and institutionalised tourists. The **drifter** has no specific destination and tries to integrate with the host society.

Table 4   Travel time and cost between New York and Los Angeles and London

Year	Travel between NY and Los Angeles (2500 miles) Time in hours				Travel between NY and London (3500 miles) Time	
	Car	Rail	Air	Min fare*	Ship/Air	Min fare*
1929	120	70	25	28	5 days	—
1949	80	65	12	19	18 hours	31
1969	60	55	5	8	7 hours	8
1979	70	—	5	5	4 hours	4.5

* Figures in cents per passenger mile in 1979 US currency equivalents.

Figure 1 The packaging of a holiday

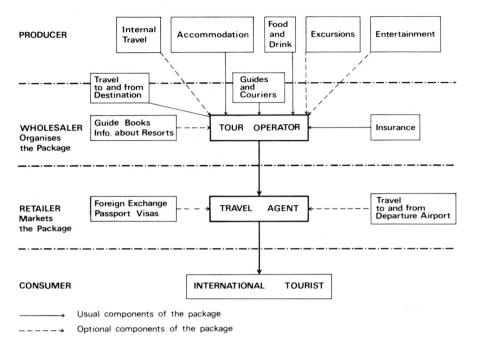

The **explorer** is more purposeful and is mainly concerned with reaching specific places. Both types of traveller are non-institutionalised tourists as they make their own travel arrangements. **Institutionalised tourists** rely on others to arrange their travel. Some are completely dependent on travel companies, even for tours and entertainment within the countries visited. Most international tourists today are institutionalised in that they make use of travel agencies (retailers) and tour operators (wholesalers) (Figure 1).

Institutionalised or 'package' tourism dates back to the pioneering work of Thomas Cook in the 19th century. As early as 1868, Cook was organising tours to Constantinople, Beirut, Alexandria and Cairo. His organisation operated boats and ran hotels. It created a system of traveller's cheques which were cashable anywhere in the world. It tried to look after every aspect of a tourist's needs. By 1880, a tourist could book a three week holiday in Egypt at a Cook's travel agency, travel up the Nile on a steamer owned and operated by Cook's and stay in a Cook's hotel in Luxor to view the antiquities. Since that time, many travel companies have followed Cook's example by trying to provide as comprehensive a service as possible.

Cook's dominated package tourism until the Second World War, using boats and trains to transport most of their clients. After 1945, it was possible to use aircraft for mass tourism. Vladimir Raitz, a Polish refugee living in London, chartered a Dakota in 1951 to take a group of holidaymakers from London to Corsica to spend two weeks under canvas. This was the forerunner of the modern air-charter sunlust package holiday. Forward planning guaranteed that charter aircraft flew with most or all of their seats occupied, thus ensuring lower unit costs (costs per person) than on scheduled flights, which often flew with empty seats. The subsequent introduction of larger and faster aircraft lowered unit costs even further.

The real boom in air-charter package holidays began in the 1960s with the arrival of jet airliners and the widespread construction of new airports in potentially popular resort areas. Ten times as many passengers travelled on air charters in 1966 compared with 1960, and many new and distant destinations were opened up. In 1966, a Scandinavian travel company transported 528 holidaymakers to The Gambia in West Africa, marking the beginning of that country's tourist industry. In 1984, over 40,000 air-charter tourists arrived in The Gambia. Airports such as the one at Monastir in Tunisia have been built especially for the air-charter tourist.

By 1971, over 50% of holidays abroad were 'package holidays'. The main elements of the 'package' are:

1 one transaction is required to purchase most or all of the package

2 the tourist travels in a group of people with similar background, interests and attitudes

3 block bookings are made for transport and accommodation, thereby reducing costs

4 couriers and guides are generally attached to the group to mediate between the tourists and the host society

5 generally the group stays in a hotel of international standard where the food and entertainment are not too unfamiliar.

The development of package tours using aircraft has made it possible for more people, especially Europeans, to take their holidays in Africa. The marketing of African holidays is very much in the hands of the tour companies. For most tourists, the main source of information on the package holidays available and the destinations themselves is their glossy illustrated brochures. These emphasise the tourist attractions, especially the three Ss (sun, sea and sand), and the 'exotic' settings. The economic and social realities are largely ignored.

The growth of international tourism in Africa

The number of visitors to Africa more than trebled from 1970 to 1985 (see Tables 5 and 6), while the number of global international tourists only doubled (see Table 1, p. 1). This relative success is partly explained by the fact that only a small number of tourists visited the continent in 1970, so any rise is likely to be proportionally significant. However, the proximity of north Africa to Europe and the active involvement of many African governments have also contributed.

Table 5 International tourist arrivals and receipts for Africa

Year	Number of people (millions)	Receipts ($US millions)
1970	2.352	411
1982	6.850	2110
1983	7.126	2108
1984	7.620	2076
1985	8.000*	2150*

* Estimated figures.

The three African countries which attract by far the largest number of tourists are all within the Mediterranean sunbelt. Morocco and Tunisia are easily accessible from the populous countries of north west Europe. In 1982, 75% of Tunisia's tourists and 57% of Morocco's were Europeans, mainly German, French and British. Egypt is not so dependent on European tourists as it attracts visitors from other Arab countries and from America. For many people, the major attraction of Egypt is its extraordinary history and culture rather than the three Ss.

Most African destinations suffer from the 'friction of distance'. Even north Africa, which is within the Mediterranean sunbelt, is further away than many competing north Mediterranean destinations. It takes at least three hours to reach Tunisia from Britain, while the Costa Brava in Spain is less than two hours away. However, cheaper labour costs in Tunisia (and Morocco) can partially compensate for the extra cost of the longer journey, as Table 7 (p. 6) illustrates.

Table 6 Tourist arrivals in African countries

	1975	1982
Morocco	1,245,000	1,815,000
Egypt	793,000	1,423,000
Tunisia	1,014,000	1,355,000
Kenya	377,000	362,000
Algeria	297,000	328,000
Zimbabwe	n.a.	256,000
Botswana	115,000	250,000
Senegal	129,000	216,000
Ivory Coast	109,000	200,000
Togo	57,000	131,000
Mauritius	74,000	128,000
Libya	238,000	126,000 (1981)
Zambia	52,000	117,000
Cameroon	108,000	110,000
Tanzania	98,000	100,000

Table 7 Comparative costs of seven day holidays in Tunisia and Spain, 1982–3

Originating country	Cost of holiday in Tunisia as percentage of comparable holiday in Spain	
	Winter package	Summer package
United Kingdom	90.4	111.9
Western Germany	69.2	102.9
France	83.1	108.0
Switzerland	71.1	87.7

Tunisia has a significant price advantage over Spain in winter from four main sending countries. It loses its price advantage in summer, except from Switzerland, but this is not so important as the demand for holidays in the Mediterranean in the summer usually exceeds supply. It is in winter when price (and climate as Tunisia is milder than most of Spain) is critical in persuading tourists where to take their holiday.

The 'peripheral' African destinations beyond the Sahara cannot compete in price with holidays in the Mediterranean sunbelt despite their low labour costs. They can provide good value for money at the resorts but the high cost of travel from Europe is unavoidable. Consequently, these countries have not become major tourist destinations. This status is reserved for countries which can be easily and cheaply reached from the main sending countries of the developed world.

Two quite popular 'peripheral' destinations are Botswana and Zimbabwe. These border the relatively prosperous South Africa, from which most of their tourists come. Nigerians dominate the flow of tourists to some of the other west African states such as the Cameroons and Togo. In contrast, countries like Kenya, Mauritius and Tanzania, in the sparsely populated areas of East Africa and the Indian Ocean, rely mainly on long-haul, affluent tourists from Europe.

The governments of African countries have often taken the initiative in developing a tourist industry. Their role can either be passive or active. A passive role means creating suitable conditions to attract investment. This entails laws to ease the transfer of money in and out of the country, providing tax incentives for investors, restricting the rights of trade unions, speeding up the processes of planning, land purchase and import licences, and trying to ensure political stability. It is left to domestic and international private enterprises to provide the money to build the hotels and supporting infrastructure. Since 1971, Egypt has followed an 'open door' economic policy in which laws have been passed to make it attractive for foreigners to invest their money there. The aim is to increase exports and stimulate the tourist industry.

During the early stages of the development of resorts, governments often find it difficult to attract direct foreign investment. Also, some governments do not want to encourage foreign investment for both ideological and practical reasons. Such investments can give foreigners too much influence over the domestic economy, and loans have to be repaid and profits sent out of the country. These situations might lead the government to take a more active role, using the country's own money to build tourist facilities. In the mid-1960s, Algeria allocated £65m of public funds over seven years to try and attract 500,000 foreign tourists annually. Part of the policy was to encourage tourists to visit some of the Saharan oases so as to disperse economic development. A government committee was set up to oversee the programme and allocate funds, particularly for upgrading accommodation in the oases.

The Algerian 'pump priming' of the tourist industry was not a great success. The oases have never been able to compete with the coast as resorts and Algeria attracts relatively few tourists compared with its north-African neighbours. Since the 1960s, the Algerian government failed to support the tourist industry consistently and its radical policies discouraged foreign investment. Tunisia, to the east of Algeria, is now a favoured destination and is featured in the brochures of many companies specialising in sunlust holidays. The Tunisian government has consistently supported the tourist industry and welcomed foreign investment. Also, it was the Tunisian government which financed the early stages of the tourist industry before it became self-sustaining in the late 1960s. The government took the risk of allocating scarce resources to an unproven tourist industry.

The governments of developing countries have received moral and sometimes financial support from international organisations. The United Nations has consistently encouraged the growth of tourism in developing countries. Tourism was seen as a vital element in the first development decade (1960–69) and 1967 was declared International Tourist Year. In 1970, the World Tourism Organisation was established as an affiliate of the United Nations. Its task was 'the promotion and development of tourism with a view to contributing to economic development, international understanding, peace, prosperity and universal respect for and observance of human rights and fundamental freedoms for all, without distinction as to race, sex, language and religion'.

The World Tourism Organisation (WTO) offers advice, carries out surveys and collects statistics. It does not invest in tourist development directly. However, the World Bank does. In 1967, the World Bank set up a Tourism Projects Department to carry out feasibility studies and recommend loans for relevant projects in developing countries. Subsequently, the World Bank has provided loans for projects in Kenya, Tunisia, Morocco and Egypt. The World Bank is a major source of financial aid and advice for developing countries. Its resources often exceed those of the smaller African nations, so its opinions about development priorities tend to be heeded, especially by countries seeking financial assistance.

Resources for tourism in Africa

Most African countries have plenty of tourist attractions. Tropical or sub-tropical locations ensure warmth and reliable sunshine. Most of the beaches in Africa are uncrowded. So, many African countries can offer the resource trio of sun, sand and sea (the three Ss) which is vital for the sunlust tourism now forming 85% of all leisure tourism. Hotel complexes are built close to the sea to exploit these resources fully.

In The Gambia, for instance, all the modern tourist hotels are built on or close to the coast, each one forming an almost self-contained pleasure area. A typical example is the Bakotu Hotel, 17 km from Banjul, the capital of The Gambia. The hotel's publicity leaflet states that it is 'adjacent to a fine sandy beach' and 'within its grounds is found a swimming pool, pool-side terraces, children's play-ground, mini-golf, exotic tropical gardens and souvenir shop'. Special 'African' evenings are organised in the hotel's nightclub. It offers a place to relax in the sun and enjoy a 'horizontal holiday', amidst luxury and comfort, insulated from the realities of The Gambia.

More and more of these pleasure complexes are appearing in Africa, where the lifestyle of the tourist contrasts sharply with that of the majority of the host population. The only 'intrusion' of local society are the 'folk' and 'cultural' events laid on to entertain the hotel guests. These help to create a slightly exotic atmosphere without disturbing the basic familiarity of the environment. Africa is made to appear to be different but not too different.

Africa has many other attractions. Some of the countries with sparse populations and few towns and cities still have plenty of space for viewing large animals. The spectacular 'big five', the elephant, rhinoceros, hippopotamus, buffalo and lion, have attracted many visitors to Kenya. Dramatic scenery has a similar appeal. There are now hotels clustered by the Victoria Falls between Zambia and Zimbabwe. Certain monuments of past African civilisations have become major tourist attractions, the Pyramids of Egypt for example. However, scenery and monuments of sufficient magnetism to encourage large numbers of tourists to travel considerable distances and at great expense are widely scattered. It is the beaches, sun and sea of the Atlantic and Indian Oceans and the Mediterranean Sea which are largely responsible for the recent surge of tourists in much of Africa.

Summary

The number of international tourist arrivals in Africa has increased since 1970 for the following reasons:

1 a great deal of money has been put into building hotels, airports and roads for tourists
2 international financial support has come from organisations such as the World Bank
3 'sunlust tourism' has been marketed aggressively in the 'developed' world
4 tourist companies have been increasingly willing to take up investment incentives. These have helped them to build and manage hotels, and to market resorts
5 the low cost of many goods and services in most of Africa helps to offset the high cost of getting there
6 many resorts in the 'developed' world suffer from overcrowding and pollution. New tourist resorts in the 'developing' countries are often still free from these problems.

In much of Africa, tourism has grown more rapidly than other economic sectors. The next chapter will examine why the benefits of international tourism are thought to be worth the costs and risks by the decision-makers.

Assignments

1   (a) Using Table 3, devise a graphical means of showing the changes in the relative importance of overseas destinations for UK holidaymakers.
(b) Why has international tourism grown so rapidly in importance since 1951?
(c) What effect did the recession of the 1970s have on the development of international tourism?

2   (a) Using Table 6, construct a choropleth map to show the distribution of international tourists in Africa in 1982. Comment on the pattern shown.
(b) Use Spearman's Rank Coefficient to test the relationship between number of tourists and distance from Europe (take Amsterdam as the point of origin). Comment on your findings. Is it valid to assume that all international tourists came from Europe?
(c) What factors, other than distance, will affect the distribution of tourists in Africa?

3   (a) What are the attractions of north Africa for the tourist?
(b) What advantages does the region have over the southern European Mediterranean fringe?
(c) Are the attractions of the region evenly spread? Comment on the implications of your answer for the economic development of the region.

2
International tourism as a strategy for development

The development context

'Give us independence and the Gold Coast (Ghana) will become a paradise in ten years'. These words of Kwame Nkrumah in 1956 reflected an optimism about the economic prospects for newly independent countries in the developing world that was common in the 1950s and 1960s. Indeed, 1960 –1969 was termed the 'Development Decade' by the United Nations, and it was widely hoped that economic progress would be rapid once the colonial ties were loosened.

Many authorities believed that the key to development lay in increasing the productivity of people at work. There were several ways of doing this: new investment in modern industrial machinery, training and education programmes; developing mineral and other resources; improving agriculture; developing transport networks. All could contribute to raising standards of living and getting rid of the desperate poverty which was still widespread.

Unfortunately, the very poverty of many newly independent countries meant that they had little or no money to invest. Poverty seemed to be a vicious circle

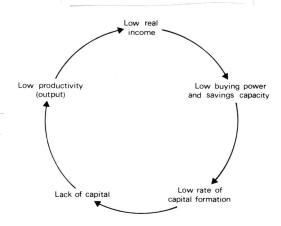

Figure 2   **The vicious circle of poverty**

which prevented the savings and investment which would enable countries to become prosperous. But how could that vicious circle be converted into a virtuous one, a situation in which economic growth, once started, could steadily gain momentum? (Figures 2 and 3)

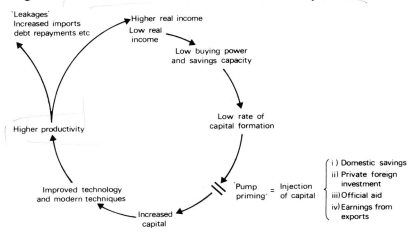

Figure 3   **The virtuous circle of economic development**

One answer was to supplement the inadequate sources of investment at home with capital brought in from overseas. Foreign aid was one such source, but many countries in the developing world looked to trade as a means of earning foreign exchange, and to selling services. One of the reasons for this was that, despite some quite large aid agreements, even by the end of the 1960s they only provided some 10% of investment needs. Also, aid was often tied to conditions which made it unattractive to the receiving country.

In addition to avoiding some of the pitfalls of aid, trade was widely seen as having other advantages. In stimulating home production of new goods it would encourage the development of skills and the exploitation of resources. In doing so it would stimulate the social changes which were also seen by many experts as vital.

Tourism as an export industry

As tourism earns foreign exchange for a country it can be classed as an **export** industry. It uses national resources to earn foreign exchange. Most of the relevant resources have the advantage of being inexhaustible: the sun, the sea, the scenery and the cultural heritage. An added attraction is that most of the tourists come from countries whose currencies are readily acceptable for world trade. Today, tourism is a significant earner of foreign exchange (Table 8).

Countries such as The Gambia, The Seychelles and Tunisia rely to a large extent on tourism for foreign exchange. However, it should be noted that the table refers to gross receipts. This exaggerates the money available to the recipient economy from tourism. Foreign exchange is needed to establish and sustain an international tourist industry. Hotels and other

Figure 4 Leakages from international tourism's gross receipts

Gross Tourist Receipts − Leakages = Net Tourist Receipts

DIRECT PURCHASES	TOURIST SUPPORT FACILITIES	TOURISM PROMOTION	REMITTANCES
Food & drink Souvenirs	Building & maintaining hotels, restaurants, roads etc.	Advertising Offices overseas	Interest Profits Wages

tourist amenities require imported materials. Money borrowed from abroad to build the first tourist hotels has to be repaid with interest. Tourists often expect imported food and drink. Foreign operators of hotels will want to send some of their profits home, and foreign workers will send some of their wages home. Money has to be spent overseas to advertise the country (Figure 4). All these constitute 'leaks' of the gross tourist receipts. The imports needed to support the industry are known as the **import content** of tourism. Governments try to plug the 'leaks' by substituting domestically produced goods and replacing foreign workers by nationals. However, especially for smaller countries, it is impossible to eliminate the import content totally because domestic agriculture and industry cannot produce the range of goods required by affluent tourists demanding a luxurious lifestyle.

The import content varies considerably, as the figures in Table 9 indicate. A relatively large country like Kenya, with a substantial agricultural sector and an expanding light manufacturing industry, can supply a much higher proportion of the tourists' needs than can a small island like Mauritius. Yugoslavia, with a much more developed and diversified economy than Kenya, needs to import very little to support its tourist

Table 8 Gross receipts from international tourism, 1983

	Visible exports ($USm)	Gross tourist receipts ($USm)	Gross tourist receipts as % of visible exports
Algeria	12,742	202	1.6
Egypt	3693	469	12.7
Ethiopia	402	8	2.0
The Gambia	45	20	46.4
Kenya	925	187	18.9
Libya	12,348	12	0.1
The Seychelles	5	33	647.1
Tunisia	1492	573	38.4
Spain	19,858	6836	34.4
United Kingdom	92,078	5539	6.0

Table 9 Import content of goods and services in the tourist industry

	Year	%
Kenya	1969	22
Mauritius	1965	90
Yugoslavia	1969	2

industry. Other factors which might affect the import content include the length of time the tourist industry has been established and the type of tourist attracted. Recently established luxury hotel complexes are likely to have a much higher import content than modest guest house accommodation.

The spread of the effects of tourism

Income from tourism benefits more people than just those involved with the hotels where the tourists stay. The money the tourist spends spreads to other parts of the national economy before it is 'lost' in paying for imports. Figure 5 illustrates this process. The tourist spends money directly in hotels, restaurants, places of entertainment and on transport. The money received by these businesses is spent indirectly on wages and purchases of goods and services. By this process extra money filters into the national economy inducing a higher level of overall spending. Several rounds of spending may occur before the tourist income is 'lost' overseas or 'disappears' in private or public savings.

The impact on the national economy of tourist expenditure is indicated by the **tourist income multiplier** (TIM). This is expressed as a coefficient —the higher the figure the longer the expenditure remains in the economy and the greater the possible spread effects. Generally the TIM in African countries is lower than in developed economies, a figure of 1 to 1.5 rather than 1.5 to 3.0, because in Africa tourism tends to increase the demand for imports. We have already discussed how tourists themselves often expect imported goods. Local people in contact with tourists often copy their consumer tastes. Young people in

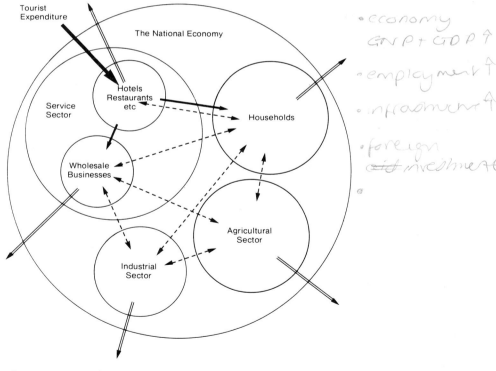

Figure 5   The economic impact of tourist spending

➤ Direct spending (via hotels, restaurants) in the national economy
➤ Indirect spending (as above) to household and wholesale sector
◄- - - - -► Induced spending between various sectors
⇐ 'Leakage' of tourist income out of the economy

11

The Seychelles, allegedly influenced by tourists, now 'want clothes that are imported and tailor-made instead of home-made, manufactured beers and spirits instead of toddy and bacca [fermented sugar cane] and English cigarettes instead of local tobacco' (de Kadt, 1979). Of course, local people have access to goods imported primarily for the tourists, and the money derived from tourism makes these goods affordable for some people.

However, despite the tendency to draw in more imports, local enterprises may well respond to the extra demand created by the injection of tourist income. A small workshop may start making paraffin stoves to be sold through the local distribution system to farmers who have profited from supplying food to the tourist hotels. The workshop, wholesalers, retailers and farmers have all gained from tourist expenditure, although none of them may have any direct dealings with the tourists. Although the material for making the paraffin stoves and the fuel they burn mean extra imports, domestic economic activity has also been stimulated.

The fact that wealth from tourism generally remains longer in larger, more economically diversified, economies does not prove that tourism is inappropriate for mini-states like The Seychelles and Mauritius. The question of alternatives has to be considered. Economic activities in the mini-states, with the possible exception of subsistence farming, fishing and the craft industry, are likely to draw in imports and the TIM might well compare favourably with the multiplier for other industries. Tourism should increase the demand for the products of agriculture and local crafts. The tourist income might not stay in the mini-state long but if it is regular and abundant it will still have considerable economic impact.

Economic diversification

In 1981, former President Nyerere of Tanzania commented sharply on the trade disadvantages faced by countries which depended on agricultural exports for their development. 'In 1971, he said, 'Tanzania needed to export two tonnes of tea to earn sufficient foreign exchange to import a Land Rover. Now six tonnes of tea has to be exported to buy the equivalent vehicle.' For most developing countries things have not improved since 1981. In addition, the price for most primary products tends to fluctuate from year to year, making planning difficult. The situation is particularly bad for those countries which depend on just one or two commodities. Kidron and Segal have identified 60 states which depend on a single primary product for over 50% of their export income.

Figure 6   Commodity price fluctuations for cotton and tea

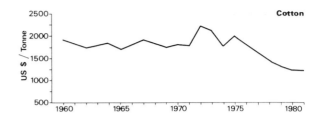

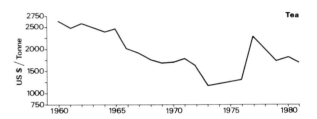

In 1969, a World Bank report stated that international tourism 'provides for many [developing countries] a useful element in diversifying their sources of foreign exchange earnings'. It referred particularly to ex-colonial countries whose exports were mainly the products of mines and the land (primary products). Primary product exporters have suffered difficulties in recent years. Since 1945, the prices of primary goods have generally not risen as rapidly as those for manufactured goods.

Figure 6 illustrates the uncertainty of relying on primary commodity exports. The real prices of cotton and tea (the prices allowing for inflation) have actually declined from 1960 to 1980. A country like Tanzania depends on exports of tea and cotton together with coffee. Many other African countries export an even more limited range of products. Kidron and Segal, in their *New State of the World Atlas*, list over 30 African states which, in 1980, relied on a single primary product for over 50% of their export income. These economies are extremely vulnerable, not only to price fluctuations but also to resource depletion and changes in demand.

Consequently, since their independence, many African countries have tried to offer a wider range of goods and services for export. The options available are:

1 to expand and increase the range of agricultural and mineral exports
2 to manufacture exports
3 to promote a service industry for which there is an overseas demand.

The first option would not overcome the problems of relying on primary production. Manufacturing for an export market appears superficially attractive, especially when it uses domestically produced raw materials, but there is no guarantee that the product will find a market, even assuming that money is available for building and equipping the necessary plant. The country will have to compete with existing manufacturing countries which have the benefit of experience, reputation, skilled management, a trained work force and a network of market outlets. The main markets will initially be in the developed countries because of their purchasing power and they might well protect their own manufacturing industries from overseas competition. African countries would also be competing with the dynamic, newly industrialised countries of Asia such as Singapore and South Korea.

Some service industries have moved to Africa because of tax advantages and the promise of limited government interference. Ship registration in Liberia is an example. However, in Africa, tourism is by far the most extensive service industry which earns foreign exchange. The marketing of tourism is already established and available through a network of tourist companies (the 'wholesalers') and travel agents (the 'retailers') (see Figure 1, p. 4). Compared with most manufacturing industries, tourism is less dependent on high technology to make it competitive. It also has other advantages, especially for a country in the early stages of economic development. If the tourist industry is successful, net economic benefits are soon realised. On average it takes only 3 to 5 years to recoup the initial investment. Some of the revenue from tourism, such as that from the sale of locally produced food, drink and transport, is immediately available for the national economy. There can be considerable delays in receiving payment for manufactured exports. The tourist makes his or her own travel and insurance arrangements, while manufactured goods have to be packaged, dispatched and insured by the exporting country. Tourism is labour-intensive, while modern manufacturing tends to be labour-saving. As a service industry, tourism thrives on a plentiful supply of labour, pandering to the demands of the tourist, while in manufacturing, overmanning can affect costs, efficiency and labour relations. Finally, tourism is perceived as a 'clean' industry, using inexhaustible local resources, and might also contribute to the conservation of the national heritage.

Some African countries have few marketable resources, especially the mini-states. Island economies such as The Seychelles have few options other than tourism if they wish to diversify their economies. Even for larger countries with more resources, expansion into export-orientated manufacturing is an expensive and high-risk choice. On the whole, manufacturing is aimed at the more accessible domestic market, saving on imports but not generating foreign exchange.

Most African countries have tried to diversify their economies from the colonial dependence on primary products. Tourism, in countries with the right resources, is seen as a relatively easy option with quick returns. Tourism represents exports without plunder.

Tourism and regional development

On the whole, tourism is a concentrated rather than a dispersed economic activity. Most tourists stay in resorts which are either towns themselves, or are zones attached to existing towns. These resorts contain various hotels of different standards, shops, restaurants, tourist agencies and places of entertainment, all served by a common infrastructure of roads and utilities. Not only does it make economic sense to concentrate facilities but it is preferred by most tourists. The average tourist likes variety and choice to be available in a resort and enjoys the lively atmosphere this creates. Already, certain African towns are becoming well known as resorts: Luxor in Egypt, Malindi in Kenya and Sousse in Tunisia.

Resort development has been used in some countries as part of a regional expansion programme. Some remote and neglected areas may have little else but tourist attractions. Algeria's 'Charter for Tourism', discussed in Chapter 1, assumed that there would be people who would visit the oases providing they could get there and stay in comfort. It was part of a wider programme aimed at developing Algeria's relatively neglected interior and diverting resources from Algiers and the coast.

Tourism supposedly provides a variety of benefits for remoter areas and can lead to further improvements. Malindi, 100 km north of Mombasa on the Kenyan coast fell almost completely into oblivion after the Portuguese moved their headquarters to Mombasa in 1593. It has recently been revived through tourism. Not only has the town grown and thrived but some of the local population have gained from the upgrading of the coast road from Mombasa. Similarly, the World Bank and the West German government (many Germans visit Malindi) have financed a network of pipelines which have improved the water supply.

However, tourism can rarely open up very remote areas. The infrastructure costs are too great and, if the region is lacking labour and services, a very high proportion of the tourist revenue would be lost to the region. Lamu, another 100 km along the coast beyond Malindi, has all the tourist attractions of the latter but only attracts a small fraction of the number of tourists. It can only be reached by means of a seasonal road and a ferry, or by light aircraft, so travel there is either unreliable or expensive. This is sufficient to deter all but the hardiest or the richest tourists. It has a few hotels and facilities but has failed to match the growth of Malindi. It remains a place for Moslem pilgrims, backpackers and rich independent tourists who have done little to change its original character.

In many African countries the capital city is growing disproportionately rapidly. Such a city is often a place of considerable cultural and historic interest but also has a large population. For example, Cairo in Egypt, already has 10 million people (20% of the country's population) living in it. Tourism can further worsen the problems of congestion and pressure on urban resources. Many Egyptian tours start and finish in Cairo, which, until recently, had the only airport used by foreign airlines. However, in an effort to divert tourists from the Nile Valley and boost tourism on the Red Sea coast, foreign airlines are now allowed to land at Hurghada, a Red Sea resort. New investment in tourism is taking place away from Cairo and the Nile Valley.

Tourism is one avenue available for a more balanced development of a country. It uses resources which are of little consequence to most other sectors of the economy. Sunlust tourism, because of its demand for a concentration of facilities and a lively atmosphere, has led to the development of towns with a specialist tourist zone of hotels and other amenities.

Tourism and employment

The other major economic argument for promoting international tourism is that it creates jobs quickly, especially as tourism is a labour-intensive service industry. Many African countries have little money but plenty of labour. About 75% of all those employed in the tourist industry are semi-skilled or unskilled.

Not only is employment created directly in hotels and restaurants but also indirectly in agriculture, manufacturing and services supporting the tourist industry. There are also jobs which are investment related in the construction and maintenance of the tourist industry. The number of jobs created per tourist bed has been calculated for several African countries. An employment survey carried out in Tunisia in 1974 estimated that for every extra hotel bed, 5.2 jobs would be created, 1.1 directly in the hotels and restaurants, 1.4 indirectly in the supporting industries

Indirect employment: a pottery workshop in Nabeul, Tunisia

and 2.7 in investment-related construction. The 56,000 hotel beds which existed in Tunisia in 1974 suggested that 250,000 people owed their jobs to tourism. However, these figures have to be viewed critically. Although labour-intensive, tourism in most countries is subject to seasonal ups and downs. An estimated 25% of the workers are laid off in the low season. It is the unskilled workers who are employed least regularly and this increases their insecurity and reduces their bargaining power for better wages and conditions (see the discussion on The Gambia in Chapter 4).

Investment-related work, although not so subject to seasonal fluctuations, is liable to fall off after completion of the resort. The Seychelles had a tourist construction boom in the early 1970s, with the building of an international airport, hotels and servicing infrastructure. After the main construction phase was complete, investment-related employment declined, though it remained significantly higher than before the boom. (See Table 10. For further details of tourist development in The Seychelles see Chapter 4.)

The clearest indicator of employment brought about by tourism is that in hotels. Between 0.4 and 0.8 of a job in a hotel is created for each extra bed. However, hotel employment, even in a country with a highly developed tourist industry, is usually only a small proportion of the total employment. A figure of 1.5% has been quoted for Kenya. In The Seychelles, however, hotels are the biggest employers outside the public sector.

The development of any sector of the economy should lead to increased work. Certain types of activity are especially labour-intensive, for example most kinds

Table 10   Investment-related employment in The Seychelles, 1970–75

Date		Number
March	1970	1500
May	1971	4000
August	1975	2750

of agriculture, and craft and small scale industries. The question is, would more jobs have come about if the money had been invested in another sector of the economy rather than tourism? Creating jobs in hotels is not particularly cheap. A study in Tunisia in 1975 found that the cost of a work place in tourism was slightly higher on average than in the manufacturing sector. At about the same time it was worked out that to provide a work place in a hotel in Kenya cost, on average, £3304 compared with £1233 in 'light engineering and repair'. Work places in hotels are certainly more expensive than in most kinds of agriculture and craft industries.

In the mid 1980s, the cost of a work place in a modern hotel in Africa was between £3500 and £7000. The figures are computed by dividing the cost of building a hotel by the number of employees. The jobs created are mainly for young people of both sexes and the unskilled, although there are opportunities for more highly qualified people. The demand for workers in the tourist industry has led to the establishment of hotel schools in some African countries. Nationals can then be trained in the skills of management, accountancy and cuisine, so that, eventually, they can replace the foreigners who fill these posts in the early stages of tourist development. The tourist industry can be quite quickly indigenised. By the 1970s, ten years after the beginning of modern tourism in Tunisia, less than 2% of the workers in the industry were from abroad.

The creation of jobs is often quoted as the reason for investing in tourism. Although, in theory, a given amount of investment might create more jobs in another sector, foreign investment may be specifically designated for tourism.

Non-economic reasons for developing international tourism

So far the economic arguments in favour of international tourism have been presented. These have the strongest influence on the decision-makers in African

countries and so tend to dominate discussions. Peters, writing in 1969, suggested five reasons for encouraging tourism. Four were economic, namely:

1   generating foreign exchange and improving the balance of payments
2   creating employment
3   the dispersal of development to non-industrial regions
4   promoting general economic development through the multiplier effect (TIM).

The remaining reason was that international tourism widened horizons and led to a new understanding of foreigners. In their pronouncements on tourism, world leaders tend to emphasise the less material benefits. In 1967, U Thant, the Secretary-General of the United Nations, introduced International Tourism Year by declaring that tourism 'fosters a better understanding among peoples everywhere and leads to a better prospect for peace'. Shortly afterwards, Pope Paul VI referred to tourism as the 'passport to peace'. Tourism was seen as a bridge between nations, leading to a better understanding and tolerance of different cultures and ideologies. However, the belief that tensions, misunderstandings and prejudice will be reduced by tourists from the rich developed countries being served by the poor of Africa, arouses a degree of scepticism!

Other non-economic reasons, besides the hope that tourism will help international understanding, can be grouped into three categories. It should be noted that all may have economic implications.

1   Tourism shows people in developing countries the material wealth, values and consumer preferences of the inhabitants of the developed countries: **the demonstration effect**.
2   Tourism projects a favourable image of little known or supposedly misunderstood countries: **image formation**.
3   Tourism encourages people to take a pride in their national heritage: **national pride**.

Demonstration effect   This supposedly contributes to the removal of 'traditional' attitudes such as fatalism and unwillingness to introduce change. These are seen by the modernisers as obstacles to development which need to be replaced by attitudes and social structures which will welcome and accommodate change. Tourism 'demonstrates' the images and values of the developed world and encourages the people of the developing countries to adopt 'modern' values. They become aware of the material deficiency of their own society and strive to overcome this through hard work and enterprise.

Image formation Many small and remote territories have become more widely known through tourism: Bali in Indonesia, the islands of Bermuda, Barbados, The Seychelles and Fiji. Some regimes which are internationally unpopular have encouraged tourism to attract sympathy overseas. It is assumed that if visitors enjoy their stay in a particular country they will speak favourably about it when they return home and perhaps affect public opinion, which might in turn influence official attitudes. Recently, two countries which have attracted considerable international criticism, Israel and South Africa, have invested heavily in tourism. The tourist trade claims to be politically neutral but it has a vested interest in political stability and public order. Political unrest soon deters the tourist. Few tourists now visit the Lebanon, once a major centre of Middle Eastern tourism. Consequently, the industry tends to favour strong regimes with open economies which allow the relatively unhindered movement of people, goods and money.

National pride Many of the new states of Africa are still trying to create a sense of national unity. They have recently emerged from the humiliation of colonialism. Intellectually curious tourists might visit such countries and show an interest in their history and culture. Increased global awareness resulting from tourism has encouraged international organisations such as UNESCO to finance the protection and conservation of monuments such as the great Roman coliseum of El Djem in Tunisia. The ancient civilisations, sculpture, textiles and music of Africa have become better known through tourism and are now more widely appreciated and copied. They create a more positive and complete image of Africa and counteract the stereotyped picture of poverty. African nations take increasing pride in their contribution to world culture.

Summary

Governments expect tourism to produce results such as more foreign exchange and jobs in order to help their national economies grow. Most African governments are pledged to achieve national economic growth. It is believed that this can be achieved by raising the output of the country's workers. To produce more, it is necessary to develop resources, new technology and new working habits, which in turn may demand new social attitudes.

Tourism utilises resources and produces a service for which there is a known and expanding demand. It is seen as a 'modern' economic activity, outward looking and progressive. Its success, however, is linked not only to efficiency but human qualities such as hospitality and personal attention. African countries have tourist attractions and a tradition of hospitality. Developed countries, particularly in Europe, have potential tourists and wealth to invest in African tourism. The combination of the two has helped to create Africa's tourist industry.

The benefits which it is claimed can be derived from international tourism have been wide ranging and in some cases rather far-fetched. However, governments of many African countries with suitable tourist attractions have been persuaded to invest scarce national resources and to borrow money from abroad to build resorts. Rarely has reality fulfilled expectations and the experience of international tourism has tended to highlight the costs and diminish any advantages. This is illustrated in the next two chapters which assess the development and impact of tourism in five African states.

Roman Amphitheatre, El Djem, Tunisia

Assignments

1 (a) Consider Table 8. Which countries are most dependent on tourism as an earner of foreign exchange?

(b) Study Figure 6. Why do Third World countries seek to diversify their export trade?

(c) Gross receipts from tourism are much greater than the actual amount of foreign exchange available to a Third World country through tourism. Analyse the nature of the 'leakages'.

2 What is the 'Tourist Income Multiplier'? Using this concept, explain how the benefits of tourism can be spread to other sectors of the economy.

3 Describe the economic and social benefits that may derive from the expansion of the tourist industry in a Third World country.

4 Assess the role of tourism in promoting *regional* economic development.

3
Tourism in Tunisia, Egypt and Kenya

This chapter and Chapter 4 contain case studies of tourism in five African states: Tunisia, Egypt, Kenya, The Seychelles and The Gambia. All five states have, with one brief exception, consistently encouraged international tourism. In all of them a tourist industry has been firmly established. Tourists travelling by air from Europe are particularly welcomed. However, these five states are located in very different parts of Africa (Figure 7). They have distinct histories and cultures. They vary in size and offer contrasting tourist attractions. As a result of these differences, they have become identified with distinct types of tourism and can therefore be taken as representative examples.

A similar format is used to present each case study, so comparisons can be made. The first section outlines the main characteristics and tourist attractions of each state. Section two looks at the development of international tourism within the state. This is followed by an appraisal of the impact of tourism. Finally, recent initiatives and future trends are considered.

The conclusion, at the end of Chapter 4, summarises the main points and highlights the problems which emerge from the case studies, referring back to Chapter 2 to reconsider the arguments in favour of international tourism.

Tunisia: a case study in mass tourism

Background

Tunisia (see Figure 7 for location) is the smallest state in north Africa, with an area of 164,000 km² and a population of seven million (1984). The World Bank classifies it as a lower middle income country with a per capita income of $1270 in 1984. It became independent from France in 1956 under the leadership of Habib Bourguiba. President Bourguiba was the leader of the Destourian Socialist Party until 1987. His party has governed Tunisia since its independence.

Figure 7   The location of the case study areas

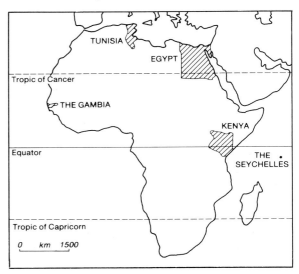

Consequently Tunisia is seen as one of the most stable states in Africa. Despite its title, the Destourian Socialist Party has consistently encouraged private enterprise and a free and open market economy. Overseas investment and foreign tourists are welcomed. Its policy is aimed at modernising Tunisia and bringing about economic growth. Despite its Arab Moslem culture, Tunisia is one of the most westernised states in north Africa, with a tolerant and relaxed attitude towards the lifestyles of foreign visitors and residents. Much of the social reform since independence has been aimed at making Tunisia a more secular society and reducing the influence of the conservative aspects of Islam.

On independence, Tunisia relied on exports of primary products. Olive oil was the main source of foreign exchange and most of it was sold to France, from which Tunisia obtained nearly all its manufactured goods. Tunisia also exported small quantities of citrus fruits, dates, wine, phosphates, iron ore, lead and zinc. Neither olive oil production nor the mining of mineral deposits was an adequate base for rapid

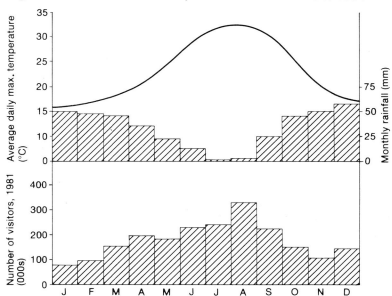

Figure 8   Climate, seasonality and tourism in Tunisia, 1981

economic growth. Olive oil exports relied on the protected market in France which could no longer be guaranteed given Tunisia's independence and the emergence of the Common Market.

In the late 1950s, Tunisia could be summed up as a country with few mineral resources, little fertile land and low and unreliable rainfall. Most of the rain fell in the mountains in the north and west, while the potentially fertile lands of the centre and south were arid or semi-arid. The government of Tunisia wished to get away from a dependence on cash crops and minerals. However, Tunisia lacked the money and large home market necessary for a rapid growth of manufacturing industries.

Tunisia is located within the Mediterranean sunbelt. By the late 1950s, large numbers of northern Europeans were descending on the Spanish, French and Italian Mediterranean resorts. Tunisia enjoyed a similar climate to these holiday destinations, with constant summer sun and relatively mild winters (Figure 8). Long, wide beaches were to be found along the east and south east coasts. However, it was different from the north Mediterranean resorts because of its Islamic culture and African location. There was a touch of the exotic which was absent in Europe. One writer pointed out that 'exoticism is what can push Tunisia in front of other sun and sand Mediterranean countries' (Malcomson 1984). Exoticism could be exploited by staging 'pseudo events' such as 'Bedouin feasts' which were adapted for the tourist to give continuous entertainment and unlimited drink!

However, with large international hotels in the resorts, there was also much that was familiar to the European tourist: the cuisine, the swimming pool, entertainment in the nightclubs, the general routine of tourist life. It was always possible to retreat from the 'exotic' to the secure environment of the hotel. Tunisia became well equipped to cater for the tourist who wanted plenty of sun in an unusual setting. It also contained many fascinating remnants of past civilisations and a vibrant contemporary culture which would appeal to the wanderlust tourist. In the south there was the lure of the Sahara. Compared with many other African destinations, Tunisia was very easily reached from Europe and package holidays were very competitively priced (see Tables 7, p. 6 and 11, p. 20), especially when the length of the journey is considered. This is due in part to the relatively low local labour and food costs. Tunisia is now firmly established as a Mediterranean sunbelt holiday destination (see Table 12, p. 21).

The Mediterranean basin is one of the most successful areas of the world for mass sunlust tourism. This kind of tourism is very much centred on the resorts, with the mainly low- to middle-income 'package' tourists generally not straying far from the hotels and beaches. Its profitability depends on large numbers (masses!) of tourists.

Development

In 1959, the Tunisian government included international tourism in its development plan to diversify

Table 11 Comparative costs of sunbelt holidays in the Mediterranean, Black Sea and Atlantic, starting from London, summer 1985

Rank	Resort	Country	Flight time (hrs)	Lowest cost (£)	Highest cost (£)	Mean cost (£)
1	Costa Brava	Spain	1¾	178	276	227
2	North Yugoslavia	Yugoslavia	2¼	201	289	245
3	Costa Blanca	Spain	2¼	201	295	248
4	Ibiza	Spain	2¼	201	313	257
5	South Yugoslavia	Yugoslavia	2¾	220	308	264
6	Majorca	Spain	2¼	216	321	269
7	Tangiers	Morocco	2¾	259	319	289
8	Monastir	Tunisia	3	262	324	293
9	Costa del Sol	Spain	2¾	254	343	299
10	Corfu	Greece	3¼	272	347	310
11	Black Sea	Bulgaria	3½	267	359	313
12	Venetian Riviera	Italy	2	261	372	317
13	Adriatic	Italy	2¼	264	370	317
14	Thessalonika	Greece	3¼	274	408	341
15	Tenerife	Spain	4¼	301	389	345
16	Estoril	Portugal	2¼	306	388	347
17	Crete	Greece	4	306	422	364
18	Liguarian Riviera	Italy	1¾	316	421	369
19	Neapolitan Riviera	Italy	2½	324	415	370
20	Rhodes	Greece	4	329	445	387
21	St. Paul's Bay	Malta	3¼	350	436	393
22	Madeira	Portugal	3½	370	423	397
23	Sardinia	Italy	2¼	355	472	414
24	Paphos	Cyprus	4¼	464	532	498
	Average			319	374	347

All figures are taken from the Thomson Summer Sun April–October 1985 brochure and refer to the price for full board accommodation for two weeks in 3T rated hotels.

the economy and increase foreign exchange earnings. Tourism would also create jobs and assist in the process of social change.

Tunisia was divided into seven tourist planning regions (see Figure 9). The Tunisian National Tourism Office was formed to prepare regional and national development plans, carry out research, regulate development and give advice. This organisation is still the main body promoting and regulating tourism in Tunisia. It has offices and personnel in the main Tunisian tourist centres and also in several major cities in Europe.

Table 13 and Figure 10 (see p. 22) show the growth of tourism in Tunisia during the 1960s and 1970s. Considering its late start compared with most of the other destinations listed in Tables 11 and 12, its achievement has been quite impressive. However, the growth in these two decades was not sustained into the 1980s. There was a considerable drop in numbers between 1981 and 1982. This was mainly the result

of a decline in arrivals from neighbouring Arab states (see Table 14, p. 23), although numbers of the longer-staying and more prosperous tourists from Europe also dipped during the 1980s, partly due to economic recession. There was also a rise in oil prices in 1979 which caused an appreciable increase in aircraft fares. Far fewer people from Britain visited Tunisia during this period. The depth of the recession in Britain contributed to this but there were other special factors too, such as the collapse of the travel companies Laker and Marina in 1982. In the previous year these two companies had transported 20,000 British holiday-makers to Tunisia. Tunisia had no control over any of these factors and they strongly influenced the number of visitors from Europe. See Figure 11 (p. 23) for the region of origin of tourist arrivals in Tunisia.

The industry now has the capacity to accommodate 3,000,000 tourists a year. However, the occupancy rate of the annual hotel capacity has never exceeded 60% and has sometimes fallen as low as 40%. This inability to fill the hotels throughout the year

Figure 9   Tourist areas of Tunisia

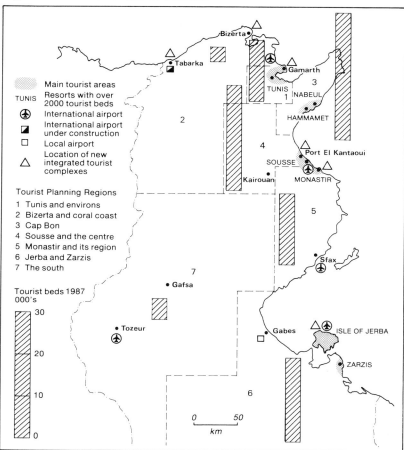

Table 12   European sunbelt tourists, 1982

Rank	Country	Tourist arrivals (1000s)	Population (1000s)	Tourist density (tourists per 1000 popn.)
1	Spain	25,291	38,230	661
2	Italy	22,223	56,840	391
3	Yugoslavia	5955	22,800	261
4	Bulgaria	5647	8940	637
5	Greece	5033	9850	510
6	Portugal	3164	10,100	313
7	Morocco	1815	22,110	82
8	Tunisia	1355	6890	197
9	Cyprus	539	650	829
10	Malta	511	380	1345

underlines one of the inherent problems of tourism — its seasonality. The capacity of hotels has to allow for the expected peak season numbers even though many will be virtually empty or closed during the low season.

Most European visitors to Tunisia are seeking reliable sun and low rainfall, so it is hardly surprising that there is a marked preference for the summer months, with nearly 50% of tourists arriving between June and September. There are also sub-peaks at Christmas

Table 13   Growth of international tourism in Tunisia

Year	Bed capacity	Overseas visitors (1000s)	Visitor nights (1000s)	Gross receipts (1000s TD*)
1962	4077	53	396	1970
1966	14,484	218	1637	13,600
1970	35,297	411	3820	31,600
1974	55,748	716	5636	80,873
1978	66,059	1141	8804	169,691
1980	71,529	1602	12,097	259,703
1981	75,847	2151	12,507	295,200
1982	80,227	1355	11,160	340,700
1983	82,162	1438	10,330	389,200
1984	84,264	1579	10,252	357,700
1985	93,275	2003	12,671	415,000

*Tunisian Dinars

and Easter, coinciding with the European holiday period but, on the whole, the winter months are relatively quiet (see Figure 8, p. 19 and Table 15, p. 24).

Compared with many other African countries this represents a high seasonality. The seasonality index is calculated by dividing the highest quarterly figure, i.e. July to September, by the quarterly average and multiplying by 100. In 1981, the seasonality index for Tunisia was 150 compared with 127 for The Seychelles and 113 for Kenya. However, both the latter two countries are equatorial with hot weather throughout the year, while Tunisia shares the coolness and winter dampness of all the Mediterranean sunbelt resorts. As long as most of the European visitors to Tunisia are sun-seekers, this uneven distribution of tourists is likely to continue.

The outcome of this is a variable demand for goods and services. In high summer the hotels are congested. In August 1981, some three star hotels (the most popular with European tourists) were so heavily booked that extra beds were placed in many rooms. In winter the hotels are often partially closed, staff are laid off, especially in the kitchens, and the restaurants and many other tourist enterprises are similarly underused.

Impact

By 1985, according to official sources, 638 million Tunisian Dinars (approximately equivalent to 600 million pounds) had been invested in the construction of 300 new hotels, two international airports and many other tourist facilities. The industry directly employed about 100,000 people. In 1963, tourism

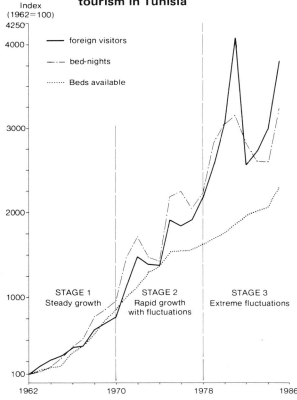

Figure 10   The growth of international tourism in Tunisia

Index (1962=100)

— foreign visitors
—·— bed-nights
········ Beds available

STAGE 1 Steady growth
STAGE 2 Rapid growth with fluctuations
STAGE 3 Extreme fluctuations

brought in 4.5% of the country's foreign exchange earnings. By 1977 this had increased to 21.5%, and subsequently the proportion has not dropped below 16.9%. After petroleum and its derivatives, tourism is Tunisia's most profitable export (see Table 16, p. 24).

Table 14   Arrivals by nationality in Tunisia

Nationality	Number of people in thousands								
	1961	1971	1979	1980	1981	1982	1983	1984	1985
French	16	132	418	366	378	361	344	371	401
West German	5	154	251	307	328	299	230	212	278
British	3	61	105	144	151	100	82	68	100
Italian	3	38	68	68	72	65	64	69	83
Scandinavian	—	32	48	53	44	43	40	60	68
Swiss	2	26	37	39	41	46	38	35	39
Begian	1	27	40	40	36	33	32	30	36
Dutch	1	15	48	40	36	34	31	33	45
Other European	2	24	53	54	60	28	46	48	56
Total European	33	509	1068	1111	1146	1009	907	926	1106
Algerian	n.a.	n.a.	184	423	897	156	256	469	770
Libyan	n.a.	n.a.	23	4	14	88	170	88	36
Rest of the World	7*	99*	81	64	94	102	106	97	91
Grand Total	40	608	1356	1602	2151	1355	1439	1580	2003

n.a.: not available   * includes Libya and Algeria

Figure 11   Region of origin of tourist arrivals in Tunisia, 1977–85

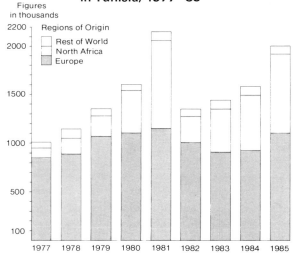

The figures in Table 16 (like most statistics) have to be treated with a degree of caution. The data for tourism refers to gross receipts and does not allow for leakages (see Chapter 2). None of the figures have been adjusted for inflation, which averaged about 10% a year from 1977 to 1985 (World Bank Report 1986). On the other hand, a considerable amount of tourist spending must remain unrecorded, especially the purchase of souvenirs from peddlars and in the souks (markets). However, the figures do indicate clearly the importance of tourism in the national economy. It is very likely that gross receipts from tourism will shortly supersede those from petroleum, as the price of oil has recently declined and production from Tunisia's small reserves is waning.

Foreign tourists stay mainly in four regions: Tunis and its environs, Hammamet-Nabeul on the south side of Cap Bon, the Sousse-Monastir region and the Isle of Jerba and nearby Zarzis in the south (see Figure 9, p. 21). Except for Hammamet-Nabeul, each tourist region is served by its own international airport. Even Hammamet-Nabeul is only a 1½ hour coach ride from either Tunis or Monastir airports. The number of holidaymakers who stay in Tunis is rather less than the figure for hotel beds suggests because, being the capital, it attracts a high proportion of business visitors. The majority of sunlust tourists gather in the other three regions, which now have substantial resorts.

An article by a French consultancy firm, *Group Huit,* claimed that the 'construction of hotels in these areas has further accentuated the coastal concentration of cities, infrastructure, industry, intensive agriculture, better educated inhabitants with a higher employment rate, and political and economic power' (de Kadt 1979). 96% of the jobs in tourism are to be found in the coastal areas and this has encouraged migration from the interior. Consequently, an **economic dualism** has emerged in Tunisia with a prosperous coastal region stretching from Tunis in the north to Zarzis in the south and a neglected interior and north coast.

A few sunlust tourists visit sites of historic and cultural importance in the interior, such as the holy city of Kairouan or the Roman remains at Dougga. Some go on a desert safari lasting from one to three days. These excursions have little lasting impact on the areas visited. The town of Monastir illustrates the coastal bias particularly well. In 1965, Monastir had three government-financed tourist hotels and was also chosen as the site for Tunisia's second international airport built with official German financial aid. In 1985, the electrified, double-tracked Sahel light railway was opened for traffic, serving the airport and linking it to the main railway system passing through Sousse. Other railways, like the line inland from Sousse to Kairouan and beyond, have fallen into disuse. Monastir is now a prosperous and well maintained town with plenty of evidence of recent investment. It was also the birth place of President Bourguiba.

New directions

The sixth national five year plan, for 1982–86, reaffirmed the government's continuing commitment to tourism. 478.5 million TD (about £450 million) was allocated for tourist development during this planning period. The main aims were to help the balance of payments, diversify the economy and create employment. This would be achieved by developing new tourist areas, 'enriching the tourist product' and by more determined promotion.

The two target areas for development were the north coast from Tabarka to Bizerta and the Sahara, using Tozeur as the access point (see Figure 9, p. 21). The north coast has less extensive beaches than the east coast and a much poorer infrastructure. However, the scenery is much more dramatic and it is not so oppressively hot in summer. A new international airport is under construction at Tabarka, extra tourist hotels are being built and roads upgraded. Similar hotel and road improvements are taking place in the south to attract more people to the Sahara circuit.

'Enriching the tourist product' means offering a wider range of activities for prospective tourists. The intention is to supplement the three Ss and encourage more visitors in the low season. The key to this policy is the building of integrated tourist complexes at Tabarka, Bizerta, Gamarth (all on the north coast)

Table 15 Arrivals of foreign tourists by month in Tunisia, 1981

Month	Numbers (1000s)	% of total
January	81.2	4
February	98.7	5
March	154.7	7
April	195.3	9
May	184.5	9
June	229.3	10
July	241.8	11
August	327.7	15
September	235.8	11
October	151.3	7
November	106.6	5
December	143.9	7
Total	2150.8	100

Table 16 Tunisia's foreign exchange earnings, 1977–85

| Product | Earnings in millions of Tunisian Dinars | | | | |
	1977	1979	1981	1983	1985
Tourism	139	219	296	389	415
Petroleum and products	166	353	664	547	569
Olive oil	26	46	50	25	43
Natural phosphates	22	18	21	27	25
Phosphoric acid	21	32	58	91	91
Textiles	65	118	163	220	283
Dates and vegetables	4	7	20	18	35
Other	203	346	451	618	824
Total exports of goods and services	649	1139	1723	1935	2285
Tourism as % of total exports	21.5	19.2	17.1	20.1	18.2

The ancient town of Sousse: looking across the Medina (old walled town) to the Katah (castle)

Port el Kantaoui: the tourist complex

and Port el Kantauoi, Monastir and the Isle of Jerba on the east coast (see Figure 9, p. 21). The complex which is most advanced is Port el Kantaoui, 6 km north of Sousse. This is a self-contained resort, centred on a marina and containing an international-standard golf course (Figure 12). There are also opportunities for riding and water sports and a conference centre is planned. Accommodation consists of high standard hotels and self-catering accommodation which is being sold to both Tunisians and foreigners. It is designed as a 'typical Tunisian village built with local stone' and 'has the charm of a typical small port'. It is nevertheless unashamedly up-market, dominated as it is by the de luxe Hannibal Palace hotel and will eventually represent an investment of over £100 million of both Tunisian and foreign money. The intended

clientele is affluent independent travellers from Europe and the Middle East. So far, the most successful innovation for attracting out of season visitors has been the 18-hole golf course. It has become so popular in winter with Scandinavians, whose own courses are weather-bound, that an extra nine holes are to be added.

The sixth national five year plan has also increased the allocation of money for the promotion of Tunisia overseas through the Tunisian National Tourist Office from 2.4 million TD to 4 million TD annually.

The government has been the main agency for the growth of international tourism through vigorous and determined action, consistent support and imagination. It has responded to the problem of overcrowded east coast resorts and seasonality and is trying to

Figure 12   Plan of the Port el Kantaoui complex

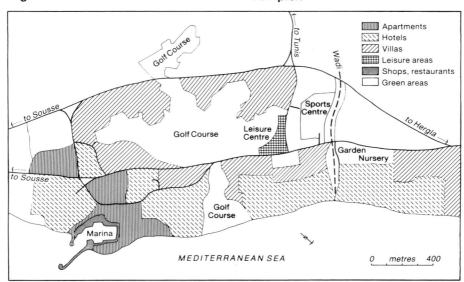

attract prosperous tourists from the Middle East. Unfortunately for Tunisia, future prospects are uncertain and the experience of the 1980s so far is not good. Few Europeans visit Tunisia for its own sake: it is merely a sunny destination offering good value for money. Only 5% visit Tunisia more than once. A survey of visitors to Sousse in 1975 found that the average hotel guest spent 22 hours a day in the hotel or the adjoining beach and 65% did not visit the town of Sousse at all. Changing fashion, political instability, price increases — all often beyond the control of the Tunisian authorities — could divert the tourists to other sunbelt resorts within the Mediterranean region, Atlantic islands or even West Africa. There is considerable competition and, except in the four months of the high season, plenty of spare beds.

Egypt: a case study in cultural tourism

Background

The chance to explore the wonders of the past makes Egypt one of the world's most desirable tourist destinations (Martin 1984).

Apart from South Africa, Egypt is probably the most industrially advanced of the African states. Its economy is relatively diversified and it has a well developed textile industry. It is also one of the main political and historical centres of the Arab world. However, the basis of Egypt's tourism is its ancient civilisation and the large number of monuments which are still preserved, particularly along the Nile Valley.

The monuments or 'wonders' include the pyramids, the sphinx, Abu Simbel and the Valley of the Kings in Luxor. They have attracted visitors for many centuries. Herodotus, a Greek who lived in the fifth century BC, remarked that 'Egypt was the gift of the Nile'. Egypt is also dry, sunny and hot, with some scenic attractions. The Red Sea has some of the world's finest coral reefs and the Sinai Peninsula, restored to Egypt in 1977, is mountainous and has considerable biblical significance.

The early tourist visited Egypt to see the sights rather than to relax. This tradition has persisted until today, especially with European and American tourists (Figure 13).

Table 17 (see p. 28) analyses the itineraries of 65 inclusive tours for British visitors to Egypt in 1986-7. Most tourists visit Cairo, the largest city in Africa and

The pyramids of Giza and the sphinx, near Cairo

a great cosmopolitan religious and cultural centre, as well as Luxor and Aswan. Few visit Sinai and the Red Sea.

Egypt attracts a substantial number of tourists from other Arab countries. For centuries pilgrims on their way to Mecca have stopped off at Cairo to visit the famous Al-Azhar University. However, in recent years Arabs have also enjoyed the relative liberalism of Egyptian society which permits a lively night-life and gambling. Some affluent Arabs, particularly those from the Gulf states, have acquired the habit of an extended stay at an Egyptian coastal resort during the summer months.

Development

Modern tourism in Egypt dates back to the time of Napoleon, but was subsequently dominated by the British, many stopping off on their way to India. The first Cook's tour to Egypt was in 1869, the same year that the Suez Canal, which boosted the number of visitors to Egypt, was opened. Cultural tourists have been visiting Egypt ever since (see Table 18, p. 28).

Tourism in Egypt has grown steadily but not spectacularly. Considering its extraordinary tourist assets, it has not fulfilled its potential. One of the major deterrents to tourists is the threat of war and civil disorder. As one commentator states, 'Egypt's present history often makes the country hard to sell, especially to those ignorant of geography'. Egypt fought wars with its neighbour Israel in 1956, 1967 and 1973. The year after the 1967 war, tourist receipts were down by 50%. Even Egypt's attempts to make peace have not always benefited the tourist industry. After President Sadat's visit to Jerusalem in 1977 there was a sharp fall in Arab tourists to Egypt.

Figure 13   Main tourist sites of Egypt

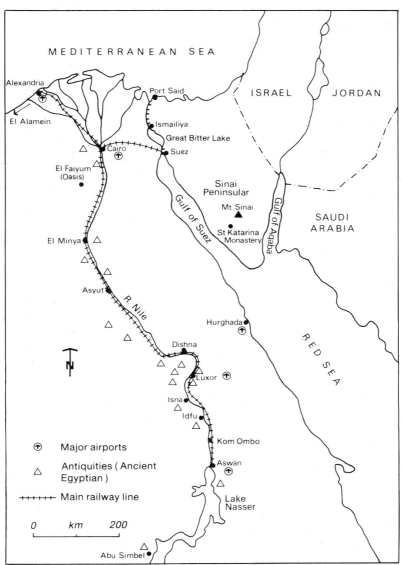

Wars have caused setbacks rather than lasting effects. Arab tourism had fully recovered by the 1980s. What is of more concern is internal security. Recently, there have been incidents directed against tourists and tourist amenities. In 1985, a fanatical Egyptian Muslim shot dead a group of Israeli tourists. A year later security forces, whose duty was to protect hotels and tourists, rioted and looted the hotels in the Giza area of Cairo close to the pyramids. The rioting spread to other Egyptian cities. It is believed that fundamentalist Muslim groups opposed to the Westernisation and secularisation of Egypt were behind these incidents.

These groups see tourists as representatives of the decadent west who must be discouraged. It is too early to assess the lasting impact of these events but they were widely reported in the press of the main source countries.

Egypt is a 'difficult' country to visit, as it requires tourist visas and insists upon complex arrangements for changing money. These measures are claimed to be in the interest of security and a way of combatting the unofficial exchange system. Better rates of exchange are offered on the streets of Cairo than in the banks. Egypt also has a reputation for being

27

Table 17 Itineraries of inclusive tours in Egypt, 1986–7

Place	Number of times on itineraries (maximum 65)	% of total
Cairo	55	84.6
Luxor	59	90.7
Aswan	58	89.2
Abu Simbel	10 (34)*	15.4 (52.3)*
Alexandria and Mediterranean	1	1.5
Sinai	5	7.7
Hurghada and Red Sea	6	9.2
Nile Cruise	43	66.2

* Many tours have a visit to Abu Simbel as an optional extra, ten offer Abu Simbel as part of the package, 24 as an option, usually flying from Aswan.

inefficient and over-bureaucratic, which can annoy and delay the tourist. These factors, combined with the heat, the relentless sightseeing of the cultural tour and the almost inevitable stomach upset, make a visit to Egypt a rigorous and demanding experience, very different from the sunbathing tourism prevalent in Tunisia.

Impact

In Egypt, 'cultural tourism' is focused on the Nile Valley, which has been described as 'the world's greatest outdoor museum'. However, the Nile Valley also contains 90% of Egypt's population of 50 million, along with much of the country's agriculture, industry and infrastructure. Congestion in this area is acute. New hotels compete for space and water, especially in the capital, Cairo.

The town of Luxor is a product of tourism. It is the capital of Egyptian tourism and is at the centre of one of the world's most outstanding groups of archaeological ruins (Figure 14). Luxor in the 1880s was merely 'a series of mud huts amidst the ruins'. John Cook, the son of Thomas Cook, laid out the modern town and built an hotel and a hospital. Today, more than any other major town in the Nile Valley, Luxor is sustained by tourism. It is full of hotels, souvenir bazaars and tourist restaurants. It serves as the terminus for most of the cruises which travel up the Nile to Aswan.

This type of 'cultural tourism' makes a particular demand on heritage resources. A lot of money is spent on the conservation of the monuments. Although this is claimed to be in the interests of mankind, the practical reason is that they attract tourists. The most famous example is the rescuing of

Table 18 Source of tourists in Egypt

Year	Arab (1000s)	OECD* (1000s)	Other (1000s)	Total (1000s)
1952				76
1962				291
1967				345
1972				541
1977				1004
1980	479	664	110	1253
1981	579	665	132	1376
1982	618	677	128	1423
1983	599	759	140	1498
1984	596	822	142	1560

* OECD = Organisation of Economic Cooperation and Development and includes most of the industrial market economies of the world.

Figure 14   Luxor and surrounding places of interest

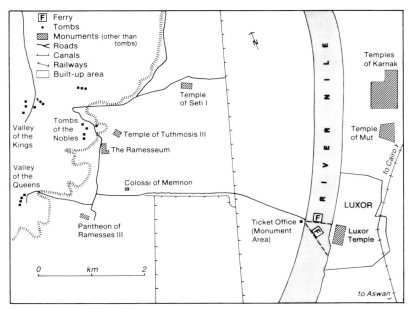

Legend:
- F Ferry
- · Tombs
- Monuments (other than tombs)
- Roads
- Canals
- Railways
- Built-up area

Valley of the Kings
Valley of the Queens
Tombs of the Nobles
Temple of Seti I
Temple of Tuthmosis III
The Ramesseum
Colossi of Memnon
Pantheon of Ramesses III
Temples of Karnak
Temple of Mut
LUXOR
Luxor Temple
Ticket Office (Monument Area)
RIVER NILE
to Cairo
to Aswan

0   km   2

the temple of Ramesses II in Abu Simbel when the Aswan High Dam was built in 1972. The operation, costing $42 million, involved dividing the statues into a thousand blocks each weighing 20 tons, lifting them 180 feet and reassembling them on a site backed by an artificial mountain to resemble the original setting. Abu Simbel is in a sparsely populated area close to the Sudanese border in southern Egypt, yet a good road and airport have been constructed to enable it to be reached by tourists.

New directions

To avoid the congestion on the banks of the Nile, tourism has taken to the river. Modern cruise boats are equipped as luxury floating hotels and are run by international hotel companies such as Sheraton and Hilton. Their functional proportions contrast with the charm and grace of the traditional *felucca* sailing boats. In 1977, there were only seven such cruisers, while in 1986 the number had increased to 82. The cruise is described as 'a unique and memorable part of most Egyptian holidays' and provides a relaxing and effortless method of reaching many of the antiquities. Day trips or longer excursions can also be arranged in the feluccas. However, the increase in the number of cruise boats is creating its own problems, as quayside facilities will soon be exceeded.

Egypt has attempted to spread its tourists by promoting three other regions, the Sinai Peninsula, the Red Sea and the Mediterranean coast from Alexandria westwards (see Figure 13, p. 27). Sinai, with its biblical significance, tends to attract the cultural tourist and the famous fifth century monastery of St Katarina at the base of Mount Sinai already features on some itineraries. However, the Red and Mediterranean Sea developments are aimed at the sunlust tourist. Here, the attractions are the beaches and water sports. The

A felucca on the Nile.

29

The monastery of St Katarina

potential for expansion is believed to be much greater for sunlust tourism than for cultural tourism. On average, only about 15% of tourists visit countries primarily to see historic sites. Cultural tourism in Egypt is, for many, a once in a lifetime experience. However, it is unlikely that Egypt will attract many people from Europe for the sand, sun, surf and coral reefs. For Europeans, destinations such as Tunisia and Morocco in north Africa are much more accessible. The marketing of these sunlust holidays is aimed more at the Middle East. Egypt feels that it could replace the highly unstable Lebanon as the main destination for Arab holidaymakers. An added

incentive is that Arab tourists tend to stay longer than Europeans and Americans (compare Tables 18, p. 28 and Table 19). However, several companies are now organising two-mode holidays for European and American tourists: one week on the Nile cultural circuit followed by a relaxing week by the Red Sea.

The average length of stay for both groups may seem rather low, but the figures also include business visitors who would normally only stay for a short time. Even so, over the years, the average length of a visit has shortened progressively. In the 1950s, when many Europeans travelled to Egypt by boat, a stay of a month or more was quite common.

Despite these difficulties, and the pessimism about the future of Egyptian tourism in some quarters, the Egyptian government continues to encourage its expansion. There has recently been a major investment of $US 1.5 billion of Arab, European and American money in a Red Sea tourist complex in Hurghada. Holiday villages have been built in Hurghada and El Alemein on the Mediterranean coast. Cairo airport has been expanded and Luxor and Hurghada Airports may now receive international flights, thus diverting some tourists from Cairo.

A new official organisation, the Egyptian General Authority for the Promotion of Tourism (EGAPT), was set up in 1981 to market Egypt abroad. In 1985, a presidential decree established a supreme council for tourism. While the State owns 17 hotels throughout Egypt, much domestic private capital has also been invested in hotels. Considerable efforts have been made to attract overseas investment and expertise. Egypt has followed an 'open door' economic policy since 1971 to promote exports and stimulate tourism.

Laws passed in 1971, 1974 and 1977 involving tax concessions, duty free imports and the repatriation of profits have created a very favourable climate for

Table 19 Tourist bed-nights* and average length of stay in Egypt

| Year | Arab | | OECD | |
	Number of bed-nights (1000s)	Average stay (nights)	Number of bed-nights (1000s)	Average stay (nights)
1980	3595	7.5	3927	5.9
1981	4637	8.0	4546	6.8
1982	4413	7.1	4371	6.5
1983	4139	6.9	4191	5.5
1984	3912	6.6	4154	5.1

* Total number of nights stayed by tourists each year.

investment by foreigners. Foreign capital has therefore been forthcoming to support the tourist industry. Americans have invested in hotel chains and Nile cruisers, the Belgian company, Wagon-Lits, operates the sleeping-car railway service from Cairo to Aswan, and the World Bank has provided a loan of £62 million to improve the tourist infrastructure at Luxor.

What is the continuing appeal of tourism to the Egyptian government? In common with many other states in Africa, Egypt sees tourism as an important source of foreign exchange in an economy and society which is volatile and changing. The Egyptian economy requires many imports, not only to help with industrialisation and modernisation, but increasingly to feed its population. Egypt finds it difficult to pay for these imports. Throughout the 1980s, tourism has been the fourth or fifth largest source of foreign exchange (Table 20).

Since 1985, remittances (money sent back to Egypt from Egyptian workers abroad) and oil exports have declined sharply, so tourism is even more important as a source of foreign exchange. Also, it is estimated that another 25 to 30% of the figure for tourism enters the black market economy, so the table probably understates the financial benefits from tourism.

The government is also influenced by the number of jobs tourism creates. Seventy thousand people are employed directly in tourism and many more indirectly. The underemployed labour force of Egypt takes advantage of tourism to offer a variety of services in return for 'baksheesh'. There is also a booming handicraft industry making and selling souvenirs. Through these means money from tourism filters into the low reaches of the economy. Most of the inhabitants of Luxor depend on tourism. So, despite the fluctuations in the number of tourists arriving each year and the need for considerable investment to improve industrial and agricultural productivity, the Egyptian government persists in supporting the tourist industry.

Kenya: a case study in safari tourism

Background

'By now there was no more road, only a cattle track, but we were coming to the edge of the plain. Then the plain was behind us and ahead there were big trees and we were entering a country which was the loveliest that I had seen in Africa. The grass was green and smooth, short as a meadow that is newly grown, and the trees were big, high-trunked and old with no undergrowth but only the smooth green of the turf-like deer park and we drove on through shade and patches of sunlight following a faint trail . . . I could not believe we had suddenly come to such a wonderful country. It was a country to wake from, happy to have had a dream . . .'

These words of Ernest Hemingway, written in 1935, helped create an image of East Africa that is still widely held today. It is a picture of one of the last great refuges for easily hunted and viewable large animals.

Like Tunisia, on independence Kenya relied on cash crop exports. Writing in 1962, H. R. Jarrett stated that 'the main importance of Kenya . . . stems from its commercial agriculture, and the chief crops grown for export are coffee, tea, sisal, wattle extract, pyrethrum and cotton, in that order'. 81% of foreign earnings were obtained from agricultural exports. The leadership considered that economic development of a poor state like Kenya required foreign investment and diversification of the economy. An 'open door' economic policy was implemented, aimed at attracting money from overseas. The Kenyan government passed laws such as the Foreign Investment Protection Act of 1964. These laws protected overseas investment and tried to limit labour disputes. Kenya subsequently became one of the most favoured nations in Africa for investment by countries such as the USA, West

Table 20 Egypt's main earners of foreign exchange, 1980–85 (All figures are in millions of £ Egyptian)

Year	Remittances	Oil	Suez Canal	Cotton	Tourism
1980/1	2105.2	1919.4	546.3	228.4	413.5
1981/2	1406.7	1914.6	636.2	204.0	317.5
1982/3	2327.5	1859.3	669.6	220.1	247.1
1983/4	2956.2	1796.7	681.8	321.3	232.2
1984/5	2835.7	1843.9	627.7	741.8	332.2

Germany and the UK. Except for the attempted coup in 1982, little has disturbed the attractive climate for investment.

Much of this investment was outside the agricultural sector, thereby contributing to economic diversification. There was an appreciable development of import substitution industries. The first oil refinery in East Africa was opened at Changamwe, near Mombasa, in 1967, supplying oil products not only to Kenya but also to its neighbours, Uganda (by pipeline), Tanzania and Somalia. However, except in the agricultural processing sector, manufacturing was unlikely to sell many goods to developed countries in the near future. Recognising this, and also appreciating the employment potential, the government turned to tourism.

The climate in the interior is very pleasant, being equable and mild because of its altitude. It is the land of eternal spring. In contrast, the coast is hot, with two distinct dry seasons (Figure 15). Expanses of white coral beach, reefs and the perpetually warm sea

(average temperature 28°C) make it ideal for sunlust holidays. The coast also contains most of the significant historic monuments, a reminder of the impact of the Arabs and Portuguese. Dhows, borne by trade winds from the Persian Gulf, are still to be found in the harbours of Mombasa, Malindi and Lamu (Figure 16).

Development

Tourism was already quite well established in Kenya before independence in 1963. This was based on the safari, though photography was rapidly replacing hunting. With the growth of tourism, conservation and animal management became major concerns. The solution was to create National Parks where the animals would be protected and the tourists would pay to visit and use the facilities. The first National Park was opened on the outskirts of Nairobi, the capital, in 1964. By the 1980s, there were 42 National Parks in Kenya. (The major ones are shown on Figure

Figure 15   Climatic information relevant to the tourist, Nairobi and Mombasa

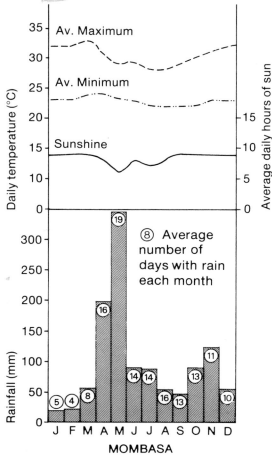

MOMBASA

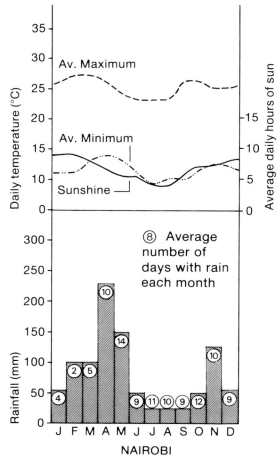

NAIROBI

16.) The largest is Tsavo which covers 13,000 km². Africa's first marine park was opened in Malindi in 1968. Here, fish, shells and corals are entirely protected from hunters and collectors. However, Nairobi National Park is still one of those most visited because it is so accessible.

In 1948 the East African Travel Association was formed to promote tourism in the region and, as early as 1950, the British Overseas Airways Corporation (BOAC) flew 50 journalists and travel agents into Nairobi to assess Kenya's tourist potential. In 1965, two years after independence, the Kenyan government set up the Kenyan Tourist Development Corporation

(KTDC) to supervise the industry and direct public investment into accommodation and transport. The KTDC works closely with the National Park Trustees, acknowledging the relationship between large fauna conservation and tourism. The fauna attracts the tourists and tourist revenue pays for the maintenance of Parks and Reserves, although tourist pressures undoubtedly cause disturbance to animal behaviour and influence species numbers and composition around lodges and campsites.

Before 1960, most visitors came to Kenya to hunt or photograph large animals. However, some Europeans living in Kenya and other parts of East and Central

Figure 16   Main tourist sites of Kenya

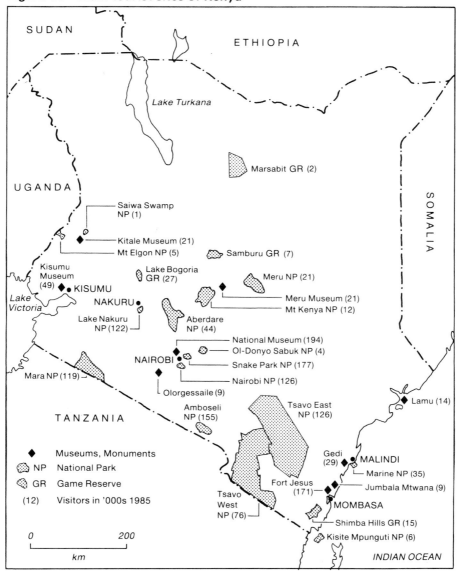

Tourists photographing animals

Table 21   Growth of international tourism in Kenya

Year	Visitors (1000s)	Foreign exchange earnings ($ million)
1954	5.3	—
1965	190.0	30.5
1970	354.0	51.8
1975	386.1	80.2
1980	372.5	138.0
1981	365.2	129.0
1982	392.1	168.0
1983	372.3	174.0
1984	462.2	217.0
1985	540.6	298.0

Africa spent holidays on the coast, usually staying in Mombasa. In 1962, a charter flight arrived from West Germany bringing tourists who stayed for the whole of their holidays in a coastal hotel. The tourist industry along the coast has expanded ever since, with Moi Airport in Mombasa now receiving direct flights from Europe.

Between 1965 and 1972, the number of people visiting Kenya rose by 132%. This led to considerable further investment in the tourist industry. During the Second National Development Plan, 1970–74, £K14 million was allocated to building more hotels and game lodges. The reason given was that tourism created employment more rapidly than any other sector of the economy. The planners assumed that one extra hotel bed would give rise to four work places either directly or indirectly. The result was disappointing. There was no appreciable growth in the number of arrivals until the mid 1980s (see Table 21), yet, globally, international tourism has risen by 6% per annum since 1970. However, a visitor's average length of stay rose from 9.3 days in 1971 to 15.2 days in 1981. Long-stay Europeans had replaced short-stay African and American tourists.

External factors beyond Kenya's control contributed to this slower than expected growth in tourism. In 1973 the price of crude oil rose fourfold. The rise in air fares meant that many holiday prices increased by 50% and several tour companies ceased to market Kenya in Europe and North America because the price was considered too high to attract many customers. Air fares per kilometre in Africa were the highest in the world. There was little incentive to develop new routes to expanding tourist generating regions such as Japan and Australia because of the overall low level of demand.

Although Kenya has been relatively politically stable since independence, the image of Kenya suffered because of events in neighbouring states. Idi Amin seized power in Uganda in 1972, heralding a prolonged period of strife and chaos there. Relations between Kenya and Tanzania deteriorated, leading to the closure of their border in 1977. The prolonged and bitter turmoil in Ethiopia and Somalia was taking place just to the north. Africa as a whole appeared to be increasingly unstable and not all Americans (or Europeans) discriminated between peaceful Kenya and the rest of Africa. *The Economist* Intelligence Report on tourism in Kenya, written in 1978, commented that 'to the Americans, Africa is a dangerous place. The trouble is they are weak on geography and international affairs. They think that Idi Amin terrorises the whole continent, the guerilla war in Rhodesia is down the road and [Kenya] is the middle of the Horn of Africa'. The general reluctance of Americans to visit Africa accounted for the decline in American visitors to Kenya. The number of tourists from neighbouring countries fell sharply during the 1970s (Table 22). There was also a general exodus of European expatriates from both east and central Africa, many of whom would have spent their holidays in Kenya. This contributed to the overall decline in visitors from African states.

Internal factors also contributed. Adverse publicity about poaching in the National Parks allegedly supported by government officials and Park employees tarnished Kenya's image. More recently, publicity about the incidence of AIDS in East Africa has been deterring visitors. In response to this the Kenyan Government has decided to open up the coast to cheap charter flights for the first time, to compensate for the generally falling numbers in the high-spending category.

Table 22 Visitors to Kenya by country of residence

Country	1972 1000s	1972 %	1977 1000s	1977 %	1985 1000s	1985 %
Tanzania	91.7	22	27.3	8	22.1	4
USA	64.7	15	33.0	10	54.3	10
UK	52.1	13	43.0	13	65.6	12
Uganda	39.9	9	9.5	2	24.8	5
W. Germany	39.1	9	51.0	15	100.3	19
Switzerland	17.0	4	25.0	7	44.6	8
Italy	13.7	3	22.3	6	34.2	6
Zambia	13.7	3	10.2	3	8.7	2
France	10.0	2	15.1	4	24.6	5
Canada	6.6	1	5.2	2	7.6	1
Other	82.5	19	102.8	30	154.4	28
Total	428.4	100	344.4	100	541.2	100

However, Kenya has relatively little control over the most important influences on tourist numbers. The majority of the high-spending, long-stay tourists come from distant developed countries. They generally have little detailed knowledge of Africa. Their holiday decisions are largely based on personal interests, social pressures, cost and safety.

Impact

The influence of tourism in Kenya is quite widespread. Safari tourism is very extensive with people travelling considerable distances. The relationship between National Parks and tourism has already been mentioned. Ideally, tourism should pay for the Parks. However, there is often a social cost in inconvenience and even hardship to some groups caused by the existence of the Parks and Reserves. Effective animal conservation and management is usually incompatible with other economic activities including agriculture and pastoralism.

Kenya has steadily increased the number of National Parks and Game Reserves while its population has also grown rapidly. The demand for land for towns and farming has risen and the cost of protecting the Parks from poachers and squatters has grown accordingly. The policy is usually to evict squatters. The World Bank loaned Kenya £3 million to improve protection of the Parks by such means as fencing. Even so, pressure for land may be so great that concessions have to be made. 2750 ha of the Nakuru National Park have been made available for resettlement of families.

Although Kenya is renowned for its safari tourism, it is beach tourism which has become more important in recent years (Table 23). Coastal tourism has led to a much greater concentration of tourist facilities than did safari tourism. Tourist development stretches along the Indian Ocean from the Tanzanian border to Malindi, with a small outpost on the island of Lamu (see Figure 17, p. 36). As a result of the growth of tourism, land prices along the coast have risen rapidly, well beyond the purchasing power of many of the local African farmers. In many places, hotels block off access to the beach. *The Economist* Intelligence Report of 1978 on tourism in Kenya noted that there

Table 23 Distribution of tourist bed-nights in Kenya

Year	Coast bed-nights 1000s	Coast bed-nights %	Safari bed-nights 1000s	Safari bed-nights %	Capital bed-nights 1000s	Capital bed-nights %
1972	932.9	38	435.2	17	1107.2	45
1977	1778.5	46	652.0	18	1407.4	37
1982	2425.0	52	802.8	18	1400.7	30
1983	2336.5	52	808.3	18	1327.2	30
1984	2418.1	52	868.8	18	1397.4	30
1985	2444.0	51	887.5	18	1486.9	31

Figure 17 The Kenyan coast

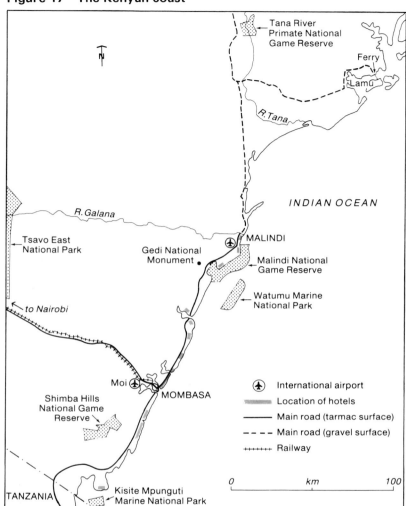

was a rise in 'beach crime' because of opportunities created by tourism. It also indicated a growing tension between local people and affluent and often insensitive visitors. The authorities reacted by removing beach kiosks and hawking licences.

Arguably, the local population has benefited from infrastructural improvements. The road from Mombasa to Malindi has been upgraded at a cost of over £K1 million, though this was a mixed blessing as it contributed to land price inflation and encouraged further speculative hotel building on what was formerly agricultural land. However, the Mombasa Water Project, which was financed by the World Bank and the West German government, serves both Mombasa and Malindi through 120 km of pipes and has benefited both tourists and the local population.

Nairobi is a sufficiently important tourist centre to merit a separate category (Capital in Table 23, p. 35). It is the starting point for most safaris as it is served by a major international airport. It has well established hotels such as the New Stanley and the Norfolk. Large luxury hotels and the Kenyatta Conference Centre dominate the centre of Nairobi. However, people also visit Nairobi for its own sake, some on official business, others for pleasure. Its wide range of shops and cosmopolitan facilities attract many Africans, who often stay with friends.

Figure 18 shows the collective preference of each national group visiting Kenya in 1985. The percentages refer to bed-nights spent in the three categories. The Americans have a marked interest in safaris and Nairobi and have little desire to visit the coast, while both Africans and Asians tend to converge on Nairobi. Europeans, with the exception of Scandinavians, much

Figure 18 Holiday destinations in Kenya, 1985: percentage of bed-nights in Nairobi, on the coast and on safari

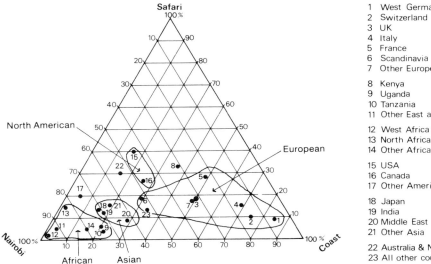

1   West Germany
2   Switzerland
3   UK
4   Italy
5   France
6   Scandinavia
7   Other Europe

8   Kenya
9   Uganda
10 Tanzania
11 Other East and Central Africa

12 West Africa
13 North Africa
14 Other Africa

15 USA
16 Canada
17 Other America

18 Japan
19 India
20 Middle East
21 Other Asia

22 Australia & New Zealand
23 All other countries

prefer the coast. To many Europeans, Kenya is now seen as an up-market sunlust destination. However, many packages combine a short safari, especially to the nearby Tsavo National Park, with a much longer beach-based holiday.

New directions

Compared with Tunisia, Kenya has a diversified tourist product based on both the beach and the safari. The major tourist initiative in recent years has been to develop Nairobi as a major international conference centre. Because of its excellent air communications, Nairobi is the most accessible city in East Africa. It also enjoys a very congenial climate and the nearby National Park is a major attraction for most visitors. The Kenyatta Conference Centre was opened in Nairobi in September 1973 (see Figure 19, p. 39). The 334 foot tower of this impressive building dominates the Nairobi skyline. The Centre can accommodate the largest international conference as it has a plenary hall which will hold up to 4000 delegates, a simultaneous

translation facility for 700 people, plus other meeting rooms, restaurants and offices. An international link-up can be arranged through the Earth satellite station at Mount Longonot. (See Table 24.)

Use of the Centre fluctuates from year to year. However, it has attracted some major, prestigious conferences organised, for example, by the World Bank, the International Monetary Fund, UNESCO and the United Nations Conference on Trade and Development (UNCTAD). The Centre cost £K4 million to build in 1973 and, according to *The Economist* Intelligence Unit (1978), the fees for its use were set so low that it was expected to take 40 years to pay back the original investment. However, the benefits exceed the actual income earned by the Centre. Conference delegates are among the highest spending tourists and usually stay at the more expensive hotels. They travel on scheduled flights, including those of the national carrier. The conferences provide free publicity for the host nation. Nairobi has established itself, along with Rome and Geneva, as a conference centre of global importance.

Table 24 Conferences at the Kenyatta Centre, Nairobi

Year	Conferences held	Conference days	Attendance	% occupancy of Centre
1981	40	263	9500	72.1
1982	29	218	18,050	59.0
1983	36	176	13,970	48.2
1984	40	160	5768	44.0
1985	35	197	28,844	54.0

Figure 19 The Kenyatta Conference Centre, Nairobi

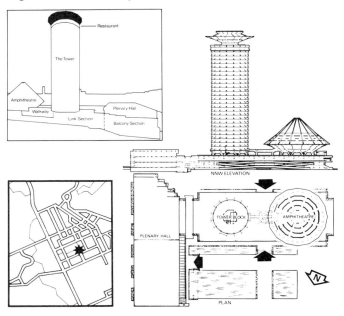

Summary

Tunisia and Egypt have both tried to introduce tourism to new areas. Kenya has harnessed its resources to attract a more influential type of tourist. This has been prompted, in part, by the relative decline of Nairobi as a tourist destination and the under-use of its high class accommodation.

Assignments

1 On a scattergraph, plot the mean cost of holidays against flight time for the holiday destinations shown in Table 11. How does Tunisia compare with other countries? Explain any differences you find.

2 Using Figure 10, describe and explain the changes in the volume of tourism in Tunisia.

3 Using Table 14, draw two pie-charts showing the nationality of tourists (i) in 1971 and (ii) in 1985. Describe and account for any differences.

4 Using Table 15, draw a graph to show monthly tourist trends in Tunisia. Comment on the pattern and describe the problems that Tunisia's tourist industry may face as a consequence.

5 Assess the importance of tourism in the economy of Tunisia.

6 To what extent has the growth of tourism served to widen regional disparities in Tunisia? Assess the work of government in trying to tackle this problem.

7 How has the growth of the tourist industry affected the urban morphology of tourist centres in Tunisia?

8 Using Table 18, draw a graph to show the increase in tourists to Egypt from 1952–84. Compare the rate of growth of tourism in Egypt with that of other north African countries and explain any differences with reference to the special circumstances found in Egypt.

9 Describe the spatial impact of tourism on Egypt. How is the government trying to spread this impact more widely?

10 Use Table 20 to calculate the percentage of total foreign exchange that was earned by Egypt's tourist industry in 1980–1. How had this changed by 1984–5? Account for the fluctuation in tourist income.

11 Use Table 22 to construct pie-charts showing the origins of tourists to Kenya in 1972 and 1985. Describe and account for the changes.

12 (a) Comment on the changing spatial pattern of tourism in Kenya (Table 23).
(b) To what extent does this reflect the particular tastes of tourists from different parts of the world?
(c) What is the government doing to make Nairobi more attractive to the tourist?

4

Tourism in two small African states: The Seychelles and The Gambia

The Seychelles: a case study in trendsetting tourism

Background

The Seychelles are located in the Indian Ocean, about 1500 km off the coast of Kenya (see Figure 7, p. 18). They are small and fragmented, with four main islands and numerous smaller coral islands. Most of the population of 64,000 (1983) is to be found on the largest island of Mahé. The islands have only been inhabited since 1770. Until the 1970s the leading export was copra, grown mainly on plantations. The plantations were owned by a small French-speaking elite known as the *grands blancs*. The plantation workers were of mixed African, Indian and European descent and spoke creole, which was based on French but had many dialect words. The islands were administered as a British colony, with English as the official language.

Smallholdings co-existed alongside the plantations. Owing to the small amount of flat land available and an inheritance system which permitted each surviving son to claim an equal share of land on the death of the owner, many of these smallholdings had become too small to provide for the needs of the cultivator and his family. Therefore, income had to be supplemented through fishing, working on the plantations, construction work and handicrafts.

The Seychelles has no known mineral wealth except guano. Its agriculture and fisheries are unproductive. Its main marketable asset is its natural beauty. Mahé alone has 64 golden beaches. There is a striking contrast between the rugged, luxuriantly vegetated, granite islands and the low lying, palm fringed coral atolls. Because of their isolation, the islands have developed an unique and varied fauna and flora, including the two million Sooty Terns of Bird Island and the coco-de-mer, the world's largest seed, found only in the Vallée de Mai on Praslin Island.

The Seychelles Tourist Board asserts that the islands are 'unique by a thousand miles'. It hints that they are the original Garden of Eden, 'unhurried, uncrowded, unspoilt', where you can enjoy 'the holiday of your dreams', since 'whatever holiday you dream of, the Seychelles can make it a reality'. The isolation of the islands is itself an attraction.

Development

The income derived from copra, vanilla, cinnamon and patchouli (used for perfumes), the traditional exports of The Seychelles, steadily declined from the mid 1950s onwards because of falling demand. Rising unemployment caused by a rapidly growing population, the return of servicemen from overseas and a stagnating economy, were linked with social problems of drunkenness, petty larceny and family instability. Many of those who had the means, including some of the *grands blancs*, emigrated. Towards the end of the 1960s, tourism was seen as a way in which the economy could be revived. Money was made available to build an international airport on Mahé so that the islands could be reached quickly by international tourists.

View towards Silhouette Island from Mahé Island, The Seychelles

39

Up until 1970, The Seychelles were visited by a few drifters, colonial administrators, businessmen and the occasional cruise liner passenger. Before the airport was completed in 1972, the quickest way to reach The Seychelles was to fly to Kenya and then travel by boat from Mombasa. From 1963 onwards, an irregular and restricted sea-plane service served the US satellite tracking station built in that year on Mahé. People tended to stay a long time after having made the effort to get there, an average of 42.3 days in 1970 (Table 25). This table also reveals the immediate impact of the completion of the airport, the number of tourist arrivals rising fivefold in a year. There was also a significant reduction in the average length of stay. British Airways started a service from London to The Seychelles which took nine hours. Direct flights were also started from other European capitals and East and South Africa. The Seychelles could be reached by those with only two weeks to spare for their vacation.

The rapid growth of tourism after 1971–72 was also aided by the general improvement in the infrastructure and tourist facilities within the islands. Between 1960 and 1965, a new road system was constructed around Mahé and in 1971 the first international-standard tourist hotel was completed. In 1972, an airport for domestic flights was built on the second most populated island, Praslin, and within two years airstrips were completed on Bird Island, Denis Island and Frégate (Figures 20 and 21).

Figure 20   The Seychelles: tourist accommodation

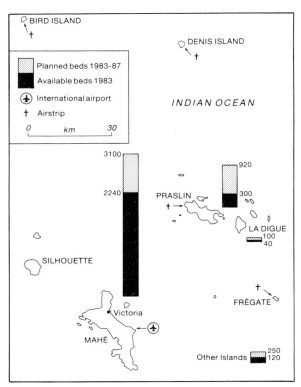

Table 25   Tourist arrivals in The Seychelles, 1970–85

Year	Number of tourists	Average length of stay (nights)	Gross receipts (SR* 1000s)	Hotel beds available
1970	1622	42.3	4855	140
1971	3175	28.5	9603	163
1972	15,197	13.1	45,728	591
1973	19,464	10.5	58,316	880
1974	25,932	10.2	72,754	891
1975	37,321	11.1	111,702	1385
1976	49,498	11.5	175,000	1870
1977	54,490	11.0	195,000	1970
1978	64,996	9.6	243,000	2130
1979	78,852	9.1	291,000	2430
1980	71,762	9.0	326,000	2560
1981	60,425	9.6	285,000	2680
1982	47,280	9.7	220,000	2690
1983	55,867	10.7	233,000	2770
1984	63,417	10.8	283,000	2840
1985	72,542	11.0	336,000	2960

* SR = Seychelles Rupee

Figure 21   Recreational facilities, Mahé Island, The Seychelles

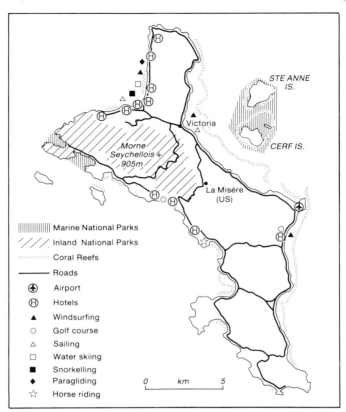

Initially, The Seychelles government, like that of Kenya, prohibited charter flights. All tourists had to arrive on scheduled flights. This and the distance from Europe ensured that only the most prosperous could consider a holiday in The Seychelles. In the early 1970s the islands became a fashionable place to visit. Visitors saw themselves as trendsetters and gained satisfaction and status from visiting, in comfort, recently opened-up, distant, 'exotic' locations.

Plog (in Pearce, 1981), writing in 1973, classified tourists according to their personalities. On one extreme were people who were self-confident, extrovert and adventurous. These he called 'allocentrics'. These people contrasted with tourists who tended to worry, liked the familiar and were generally ill at ease away from home. These he called 'psychocentrics'. The personality of most travellers fell somewhere between these two extremes. However, it was the rich and adventurous who first moved into distant destinations such as The Seychelles. They were the spearhead of mass tourism. In the normal course of events many more tourists would follow their example and visit the 'discovered' destination. When this happened the adventurous would move on to another 'unspoilt'

destination. However, if the price remained too high the second expanding phase of mass tourism might not occur in these new centres. The destination would remain, at best, a high-cost exclusive resort. Figure 22 shows the normal distribution of the population with different personalities as argued by Plog, and the destinations which might appeal to each personality type living in London in the mid 1970s.

Political change, unrest and, for a time, official indifference to tourism contributed to the slump in the early 1980s. In 1977, the first leader of the independent Seychelles was overthrown in a coup by the left wing Albert René. Although this had no immediate impact on arrivals, the new administration feared that tourism would reduce the people of the island to a new class of servants, barmen and waitresses. The 1980–84 development plan only allocated 1% of public investment to tourism and overseas investors were discouraged by the attitude of the government. There were other reactions to the coup including student unrest over a proposed national youth service. The most publicised incident was the mercenary attack which attempted to overthrow René in November 1981 but which got no further than Mahé Airport.

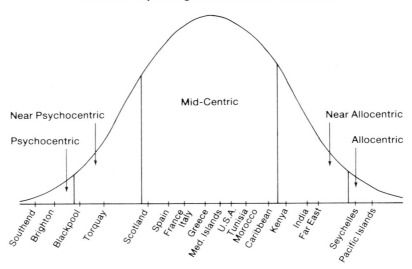

Figure 22   Selected destinations according to personality of the traveller departing from London, UK, in the 1970s

Near Psychocentric

Psychocentric

Mid-Centric

Near Allocentric

Allocentric

Southend Brighton Blackpool Torquay Scotland Spain France Italy Greece Med. Islands U.S.A. Tunisia Morocco Caribbean Kenya India Far East Seychelles Pacific Islands

However, the gun battle between the mercenaries and the security forces was witnessed by arriving and departing tourists and the damage to tourism was estimated at $2 million. An Air India aircraft flying in from Zimbabwe was commandeered by the mercenaries so that they could escape to South Africa. These events, together with the rising cost of fuel, persuaded British Airways to abandon its direct link between Mahé and London in 1982. Air Malawi, which had up to this time transported many South African visitors, also withdrew. The declining demand did not warrant these services but without them tourists could not reach The Seychelles.

Impact

Table 26 illustrates how conspicuous tourists must be in The Seychelles, even in the slump year of 1982, compared with much more spacious and populated countries.

On small islands the economic and social impact of tourism can be sudden and far reaching. Table 27 shows how tourism has replaced plantations as the dominant export sector in recent years. It also shows clearly The Seychelles' dependence on tourism for foreign exchange (compare this with Tunisia, Table 16, p. 24). In addition, in 1983, tourism contributed 50% to the Gross Domestic Product (a measure of the country's income) and provided 35% of government revenue and 15% of waged employment. The original plantation economy has been almost totally eclipsed, although cinnamon and coconut products are still beind exported. The rise and fall of tourist arrivals is now used to gauge the health of the economy rather than the harvest and market for cash crops.

Tourism dominates the commercial economy. It earns and employs more than any other sector. The construction boom, from 1969 to 1974, which launched international tourism, created jobs for able-bodied men. Many women found work in the new

Table 26   Comparison of tourist concentration in African countries, 1982

State	Population (1000s)	Area (km²)	Coastline (km)	Tourists	Tourist density	Tourists/km²
The Seychelles	64	443	491	47,000	738	106
Egypt	44,500	1,001,000	2450	1,423,000	32	1.4
The Gambia	640	11,369	80	31,000	48	2.7
Kenya	18,780	582,646	536	362,000	19	0.6
Tunisia	6890	164,000	1143	1,355,000	197	8

Table 27 Export earnings from The Seychelles, 1985: visibles and tourism compared

Commodity	Export earnings ($US million)
Copra	1.25
Cinnamon bark	0.17
Fish	1.55
Coconuts	0.03
Others	0.27
Total visible exports	3.27
Tourism	31.00
Tourism as % of visible exports	948%

Table 28 Expenditure by visitors to The Seychelles, 1984

Item (RS million)	Expenditure
Hotel receipts	
Large hotels	136.6
Small hotels, guest houses	32.2
Other expenditure	
Restaurants	23.3
Car hire	13.0
Taxis and buses	4.8
Excursions	21.9
Handicrafts	15.8
Other shopping	11.6
Unallocated	22.6
Prepayments	5.6
Expenditure from cruise-ship and short-stay transit passengers	2.0
Less estimated receipts from Seychellois in hotels	−5.1
Total income from tourism	284.3

hotels. Unemployment disappeared in the space of a couple of years. However, full employment was not sustained. Male unemployment has reappeared because of the decline in construction and the tourist industry tends to shed labour rapidly when the number of arrivals drop. In 1979, when a record number of 78,852 tourists visited The Seychelles, the industry employed 3370 people directly and 8000 indirectly. The annual occupancy rate of the hotels was 64%. Four years later the number of visitors had declined to 55,867 and the occupancy rate to 48%, with a consequent fall in employment to 2560 direct and 6100 indirect.

Tourism, through the spread effects (see Chapter 2), should benefit people other than those with whom it has direct contact. However, benefits do not appear to have reached all members of Seychellois society. The urban and rural poor have suffered rather than gained, particularly because of the rise in the price of fish, the main source of protein.

Tourism in The Seychelles tends to favour the large-scale, often foreign controlled enterprise, rather than the small-scale domestic one. The small-scale domestic enterprises in Table 28 are the 'small hotels and guest houses' and 'handicrafts', with possibly a few restaurants, taxis and shops. Tourists on prearranged packages invariably stay in large 'international' hotels. The occupancy rate of such hotels in 1984 on Mahé was 61%, while for guest houses it was only 23%. However, local craft work has received some stimulus, especially raffia work and shell preparations.

The tourist industry is for foreigners. Few Seychellois stay in the hotels, so they are designed and run to cater for predominantly European tastes (see Table 29, p. 44, for main countries of origin of the tourists). The tourist industry also imports much of the food it requires. Local fishermen and farmers have been unable to increase production adequately despite higher prices. Fresh fish and vegetables are flown in regularly from Kenya. In 1973, the value of imported goods was nine times greater than in 1963. It is estimated that 60% of gross receipts 'leak' to pay for the imports necessary to support the tourist industry.

The other element which is largely imported is capital. Tax concessions encouraged the inflow of international capital in the early 1970s and much of this money was used to buy land suitable for hotels, restaurants and other tourist facilities. This also happened to be the best agricultural land, thus restricting even more the possibility of increasing agricultural production. By 1973, over 20% of the land was owned by foreigners, as were all major hotels, game fishing boats, charter yachts and car rental agencies. This monopoly has been broken subsequently, mainly through government intervention, but overseas money and interests still dominate the industry.

Women find it easier to obtain jobs in the hotels than men. Many hope to form a permanent liaison with a tourist to improve their financial and social status.

43

Table 29 Tourist arrivals in The Seychelles, 1985

Country of residence	Number of tourists	Arrivals per week	Direct flights (Airlines)
France	12,174	2	Air France
UK/Eire	9837	3	{ Air Seychelles { British Airways
Western Germany	10,085	1	Air Seychelles
Italy	11,444	2	Air Seychelles
Switzerland	5637	1	Swissair
Austria	1024	0	(No direct flights)
Benelux	1631	1	Air Seychelles
Other European	3921	0	(No direct flights)
Reunion	1744	2	Air France
Mauritius	569	2	{ Air France { Air India
East Africa	1885	3	Kenya Airways
South Africa	2001	1	British Airways
Other Africa	1786	0	(No direct flights)
Middle East	1425	3	{ Air France { Air Seychelles
Indian subcontinent	568	2	{ Air India { British Airways
Hong Kong	574	1	British Airways
Japan	4065	1	British Airways
Other Asian	786	0	(No direct flights)
Oceania	502	0	(No direct flights)
America	1884	1	British Airways*
Total	72,542		

* This is a stopover in Anchorage, Alaska en route from London to Johannesburg via The Seychelles.

This, and the growing feeling that working in the tourist industry is undignified, has led to growing resentment:

'In Victoria [the capital], groups of half-sullen youths, Afro haircuts over T-shirts and jeans, hang about the little town centre, staring with faint aggression at British, European and South African tourists bustling happily among the handicraft shops. They have part-time jobs or no jobs at all, while their girlfriends, or the girls to whom they aspire, are waitresses in the hotels, earning as much or more than they do. They are bored and suffer from the feelings that they have been demeaned.' (Martin Wollacote, *The Guardian*, October 1975).

Often the poor and the young men feel alienated. In addition, tourism has contributed to an awareness of their deprivation. Not only has tourism shown them the lifestyle of developed countries but it has influenced new consumer tastes among the Seychellois.

The Seychellois, including the *grands blancs*, had neither the money nor the contacts to develop a modern international tourist industry. The 1969–74 construction boom revealed a skill gap, which was overcome by employing overseas workers. By 1973, 517 foreigners were working in The Seychelles, over 5% of the workforce. Most of these were in positions of responsibility in the tourist industry, running hotels, yacht and car hire firms and restaurants. Ten years later, the number had risen to 600, managing mainly tourism and light industry. In terms of economic power they had supplanted the *grands blancs*. Political power has been passed on to the mixed race majority through political changes introduced since 1967.

New directions

The Government response to a fall in the number of visitors in the early 1980s was to permit charter flights and inaugurate its own airline, Air Seychelles. Air Seychelles provided direct links with London, Frankfurt, Amsterdam and Rome. With a community as small as that of The Seychelles, there is only tourism to justify long-haul air-links, yet tourists will only visit the islands if fast and direct transportation is available. Air travel and international long distance tourism are inextricably linked. For small nations like The Seychelles, tourism sustains many of its external and internal air routes.

The availability of direct flights, the size of the population and affluence of the source country influence the national distribution of arrivals. The scheduled flights listed above are supplemented by charter flights from the main sending countries. The air route network shows a distinct corridor between Western Europe and The Seychelles and a much shorter one between Kenya and The Seychelles. Links with other areas are very restricted or non-existent. Nearly all the links exist because of tourism.

The economic crisis and unemployment of the early 1980s forced the government to look more favourably on tourism. In the 1984–88 Plan, tourism was reinstated as a major component in the government's development strategy. The target was to increase the beds available from just under 3000 to 4370 by 1988, and to attract 95,000 visitors spread as evenly as possible throughout the year so that there would be no more than 4000 visitors on the islands at one time (see Figure 20, p. 40). More emphasis would be given to islands other than Mahé. Silhouette was to acquire its first hotel. The tourist industry as a whole would be upgraded in terms of quality of service and accommodation, so that it could continue to compete effectively on the world market.

The government is still concerned about the impact of international tourism and the image of The Seychelles abroad. Tourist literature is forbidden from using 'sex or any other undignified symbols'. It should tell the tourist about social and economic development. However, as The Seychelles still require foreign exchange, they have no option but to persevere with tourism. Without foreign exchange many of the goods which the islanders are now used to would no longer be available. The economy would largely revert back to subsistence farming and fishing. The government could try to distribute tourist investment and revenue more fairly but could not accept the consequences of doing away with it.

The Gambia: a case study in winter sun tourism

Background

The Gambia, with a population of much less than one million and a land area of under 10,000 km², is one of the smallest countries on mainland Africa. It is, however, appreciably larger than The Seychelles. It stretches for 480 km along the Gambia River. Nowhere is it more than 50 km across. On all sides except for the short Atlantic coast, it is surrounded by Senegal (Figure 23).

Groundnuts have been the main export since the abolition of the slave trade in the early 19th century. On average, they have earned 90% of The Gambia's foreign exchange each year. The nation's income, the government's revenue (mainly derived from an export

Figure 23 The Gambia

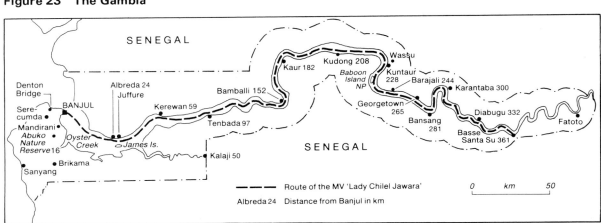

Figure 24 Climate and tourism in The Gambia

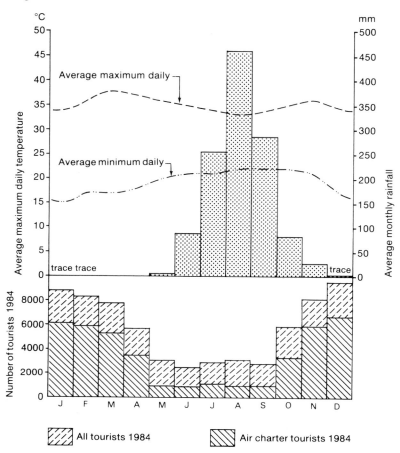

The Aboko Nature Reserve, The Gambia

tax), and the wealth of the farmers have all fluctuated with the rise and fall of the price of groundnuts.

The British colonial administration tried to find additional products to export. Cotton, tropical hardwoods, rubber and, for a brief period between 1956–59, ilmenite, a mineral used in the manufacture of white paint, were all tried without much success. In 1964, on the eve of independence, The Gambia was described as a 'non-viable monoculture', thus emphasising the narrowness and weakness of its economy.

The Gambia's main tourist assets are its winter sun and its relative closeness to Europe compared with East Africa and the Caribbean. The winter months are almost completely dry with high daily temperatures (Figure 24) but refreshingly cool evenings and nights. The Gambia Hotel Association brochure sums up the winter appeal of The Gambia: 'You needn't go as far as the Caribbean in search of winter sun. Gambia is much closer to home (i.e. Britain). Between November and May this little country on the coast of West Africa has the perfect climate with day after day of cloudless skies and tropical sunshine virtually guaranteed'.

The one great natural feature of The Gambia is its river (see Figure 23, p. 45). It provides the habitat for over 400 species of birds and is the home of crocodiles and hippopotami. The history of The Gambia is focused on its river. There are stone circles dating back 1200 years at Wassau, and European colonial forts at Barra Point, Albreda and Fort James. The village of Juffure is now celebrated as the home of Kunta Kinteh, who was abducted by slavers 200 years ago. He became widely known through the best selling book and television series *Roots*, written by the slave's American descendant Alex Haley.

Development

The growth of modern international tourism in The Gambia started when the country became independent in 1965 (see Table 30). It represented the latest attempt to find an extra source of foreign exchange. Unlike The Seychelles or Kenya, The Gambia has sought from the outset to attract the mass package tourist travelling on a chartered aircraft. The industry made a slow start in the late 1960s, with the Swedish firm Vingressor Club 33 being the only travel company to organise package holidays to The Gambia for four years. Most visitors came from Scandinavia until the late 1970s when more European companies started marketing The Gambia as a tourist destination. Now the majority of visitors come from the UK (see Table 31, p. 48). Since 1975–76, total numbers have tended to fluctuate as tourists have reacted to price increases (such as that caused by the rise in oil prices in 1979) and political instability (there was a well-publicised but abortive coup in 1982) (Table 30).

Another feature of the Gambian tourist industry is its extreme seasonal concentration (see Table 32, p. 48). The first air charter group set the pattern by arriving in December 1965 and The Gambia has until recently been marketed in Europe as a winter sun destination. The summer, which is hot and wet, is much more difficult to sell to European tourists. During this season it competes with the hot, dry Mediterranean resorts which are cheaper and much easier to reach from northern Europe.

Almost all the tourist hotels are foreign owned. The Gambian government offers generous incentives to foreign investors. These include tax free imports of building materials for hotels and of alcohol, soft drinks and food for use in hotels and no taxation on profits for five years. During 1975–80 there was a major tourist infrastructure project, supported by a $9.2 million loan from the African Development Bank, the World Bank and West Germany. Yundum Airport, 30 km from Banjul, was enlarged so that it could be used by the largest airliners.

Table 30 Growth of international tourism in The Gambia

Year	Air charter tourists[1]	All charter tourists[2]	Non-charter tourists[3]	Number of tourist hotels	Number of tourist beds[4]
1965–66	300	—	—	2	52
1970–71	2601	—	—	6	404
1971–72	8031	—	—	10	1012
1972–73	15,584	20,688	—	10	1509
1973–74	20,383	24,766	—	13	1883
1974–75	18,651	23,805	3130	14	1905
1975–76	21,116	25,287	4215	13	1997
1976–77	19,505	25,928	9022	14	2147
1977–78	15,769	21,738	9875	13	2128
1978–79	25,907	31,389	12,905	13	2291
1979–80	23,822	26,587	16,165	15	3012
1980–81	19,209	22,391	14,879	16	3360
1981–82	13,331	17,152	15,686	16	3420
1982–83	26,745	29,946	14,695	16	3989
1983–84	39,491	43,244	20,864	16	3927
1984–85	45,961	49,328	24,525	16	3865

[1] Figures are given for the period starting in July one year and ending in June the next.
[2] 'All charter' includes tourists travelling by land from neighbouring Senegal.
[3] This figure refers to all overseas arrivals in The Gambia regardless of the reason for the visit.
[4] Number of hotel bed rooms available vary according to maintenance and refurbishing requirements.

Table 31 Air charter tourists to The Gambia according to nationality

Nationality	1974–75	%	1984–85	%
Swedish	11,082	59	5911	13
Danish	5125	27	2636	6
Norwegian	705	4	701	2
German	534	3	2106	5
British	362	2	23,742	51
Finnish	344	2	669	1
Swiss	12	—	1414	3
French	—	—	4330	9
Other	499	3	4352	9
Total	18,651	100	45,861	100

By the 1980s enough accommodation had been built for the anticipated number of tourists. According to *The Economist* Intelligence Unit, there were 'no deficiencies in the basic tourist provision other than electricity supply' (1983).

The Gambian government has declared that it does not want a tourist industry which is of 'unmanageable' size and still sees agriculture as its top development priority. Table 30 (p. 47) shows that no new tourist hotels were built from 1980 to 1985.

Impact

The marked seasonality has a significant impact on the pattern of employment in tourism in The Gambia.

Table 32 Air charter tourists arriving in The Gambia each month

Month	1981	1984
January	3886	6104
February	3509	5933
March	3235	5336
April	1597	3563
May	0	774
June	0	738
July	0	1164
August	0	927
September	0	955
October	46	3324
November	2323	5884
December	2343	6659
Total	16,939	41,361
Seasonality index	251	168

Some 3000 people are directly employed in tourism, about 10% of the country's wage earners. Only about 50% are employed full time, the remainder are hired on a casual basis. The casual worker is not protected by minimum wage legislation and can be readily hired and laid off. The tourist industry also sustains a wide range of small scale activities. These include the production and sale of handicrafts and transport (especially taxi cabs). They are usually individual or family enterprises and earnings are irregular. Some of these activities are now totally dependent on tourism. Many cobblers are now making leather goods for the tourist as the domestic market for shoes has been captured by cheaper plastic imports from China. Many craft stalls close down in the summer, selling their stock and assets to survive during the low season and then borrowing money to set up for the new season. Taxi drivers' takings in the summer are half those in the tourist season. The so-called 'professional friends' who importune tourists and offer a variety of services in return for 'gifts' join the ranks of the semi-educated young male unemployed.

Figure 25 (p. 50) shows that tourism in The Gambia is centred on the Atlantic beaches in and close to the capital, Banjul. This is where almost all the tourist facilities are to be found. Official statistics showing the participation rates of package tourists in organised excursions are summarised in Table 33. These figures obviously under-report tourists visits to some destinations but they suggest their relative popularity. Unsurprisingly, the most popular excursions are to places within 50 km of Banjul and are concerned with general sightseeing and shopping and avoid an overnight stay. The figures reinforce the impression that tourism is concentrated on this one area of The Gambia close to the capital and the international airport. Here the resources for sunlust holidays are available in abundance. In contrast, the one great natural feature of The Gambia and the scene of much of its history, the Gambia River, has failed to become a significant tourist attraction, except at its estuary near Banjul.

New directions

The two weaknesses of Gambian tourism are its seasonal and spatial concentration. Attempts have been made to extend the season with a limited amount of success. The figures for 1984 in Table 32 show an increasing number of summer tourists taking advantage of significant discounts. However, the weather in summer deters most sunlust tourists and all the major international tour operators still confine their marketing of The Gambia to the winter months. Most groups arriving in the summer are 'special interest' groups who wish to study some aspect of The Gambia.

The Ministry of Tourism has recently tried to attract international conferences to The Gambia, recommending the summer months when the prices are low and there is no congestion. However, conference facilities are limited and during 1984–85 there was only an average of one conference each month. The largest conference hall can only accommodate 200 and there is nothing comparable to the Kenyatta Conference Centre in Kenya.

It was hoped that Alex Haley's *Roots* would lead to a tourist bonanza for The Gambia. The Gambian connection has been emphasised in the official tourist literature:

'It was in the tiny village of Juffure, about 32 km from Banjul on the north bank of the River Gambia, that in 1767 a young Gambian disappeared and was never to be seen again by his family and friends. But he was never forgotten since his name was passed on from one generation to another . . . 200 years later author Alex Haley was able through his researches to prove that his great great grandfather was called Kunta Kinteh who was abducted from Juffure and sold into slavery.'

Anticipating demand from black Americans for 'Roots tours', 'Reunion tours' and 'Pilgrimage to the motherland tours', the Gambian government opened a tourist office in New York. The village of Juffure is to be preserved as a national monument so that visitors can visit the home of the Kinteh family and see 'exactly how Gambians in this part of the country lived 200 years ago'.

Table 33   Tourist excursions in The Gambia

Excursion	Length	Years offered[1]	Number of years	Number of tourists	Average number of tourists for each year offered	% of air charter tourist period offered
City tour[2]	½ day	72/3–84/5	13	121,524	9348	40
Gambia Safari[3]	1 day	78/9–84/5	7	39,878	5697	20
Abuko Game Reserve and Brikama Village	½ day	72/3–84/5	13	39,972	3074	13
Creek tour[4]	1 day	79/9–84/5 (ex.82/3)	6	22,395	3732	13
Boat trip, Gambia River estuary	½ day	81/2–84/5	3	7097	2366	9
James Island/ Juffure	1 day	78/9–84/5	7	15,926	2275	8
Wrestling at Serrekunda	½ day	79/80–84/5	6	9822	1637	6
Tendaba	2 day	72/3–84/5	13	18,585	1430	6
Kafountine[5]	1 day	80/1–84/5	5	5061	1012	5
Basse	3 day	78/9–82/3	5	2810	562	2

[1] Records start 1972/3
[2] Banjul, Albert Market, Kanifung Industrial Estate, Serrekunda
[3] Along the coast to the south including stops at beaches and village
[4] By boat from Denton Bridge to Mandinari Village and return
[5] Southern Senegal
For locations see Figure 25.

In 1978–79, Juffure, within easy reach of Banjul, became part of the official tourist circuit. The one-day excursion offers a boat ride across the Gambia River's estuary and a combined visit to Juffure and the nearby 17th century fort on St James Island. However, as Table 33 (p. 49) shows, less than 10% of the air charter tourists make the trip; mangrove swamps, the great river, the history of slavery and rural Africa have to compete with the uncluttered and easily reached beaches of the Atlantic coast.

The Gambian government has been even less successful in attracting Americans to 'Roots' and similar tours. Only a few 'Roots' tourists visit The Gambia each year and hardly any come on air charter tours (see Table 34). There is no direct air service from North America to The Gambia and the demand has been insufficient to warrant the organisation of charter flights. The tourist office in New York has subsequently been closed. Juffure remains on the fringe of the tourist area centred on Banjul and the Gambian Atlantic coast.

The Gambia River is looked upon as a potential tourist resource (see Figure 23, p. 45). Recently Gambian River cruises have been made available. In 1978, the M.V. *Lady Chilel Jawara* was launched. This boat was named after the President's wife and had accommodation for 40 first class passengers. Although intended for general passenger and freight service, the *Lady Chilel* departed every Tuesday from Banjul for Basse in the tourist season, the return journey taking four days. However, in summer it made the journey only once a month since the Gambians preferred the speed and convenience of the all weather road now open along the south bank of the river.

The *Lady Chilel* sank in 1985 but is to be replaced. However, there are still private yachts to be hired and these are often chartered by tourist companies for long periods during the high season. These companies offer cruises lasting several days as part of a package. One British-based tour operator advertises '4 to 7 day cruises into real Africa with a stay at a first class beach hotel on board the British crewed yachts *Spirit of Galicia* and *African Spirit*'. These hybrid packages, modelled on the Kenyan beach and safari holidays, cost 50% to 100% more than one-centre coastal holidays for the equivalent period. Only a small number of tourists go on them.

Figure 25   Concentration of tourists in The Gambia

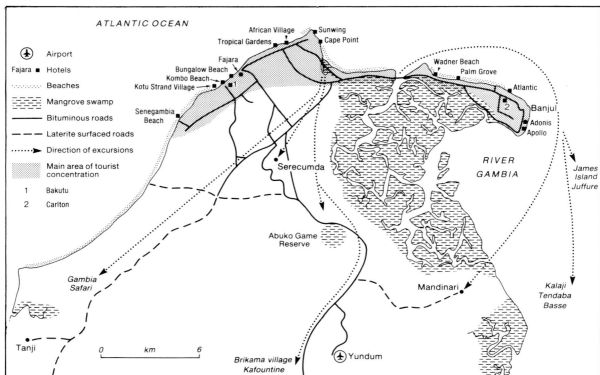

Table 34 Number of Americans visiting The Gambia as air charter tourists

Year	Number of US air charter tourists	Total air charter tourists
1977–78	38	25,907
1978–79	120	23,822
1979–80	83	19,209
1980–81	55	13,331
1981–82	90	26,745
1982–83	176	39,491
1983–84	256	45,861

The journey up the Gambia River is full of interest, especially to the observant and discerning tourist, but it cannot be compared with the Nile trips. There is nothing sufficiently dramatic to draw people away from the Atlantic beaches for more than a brief excursion. Even *Roots* has failed to arouse the curiosity of the European sunlust tourist. Black Americans who might identify with the story of Kunta Kinteh find The Gambia and its river too difficult to reach. As long as winter sun holidays dominate, few tourists will see more than the estuary. The upper reaches will remain as remote as the Sahara is to many of the tourists who visit the beaches of Tunisia and Morocco. The tourist areas will continue to be a core around Banjul and the adjacent coast; a fringe, reachable within a day on an organised excursion; and a periphery, distant and lacking tourist facilities.

Assignments

1 (a) Use Table 25 to construct a line graph showing the volume of tourism in The Seychelles from 1970 to 1985.
(b) Describe and account for the fluctuations shown.
2 Use data from Table 29 to construct a choropleth map of the origins of tourists to The Seychelles. Describe and explain the pattern.
3 (a) Assess the importance of tourism in the economy of The Seychelles.
(b) What social and economic problems have resulted from the growth of tourism?

(c) Account for the changes in official policy towards tourism in the mid 1980s.
4 (a) Describe the tourist assets possessed by The Gambia.
(b) Describe the seasonal pattern of tourism in The Gambia and assess its effects on the labour market.
(c) Describe the spatial distribution of tourist facilities in The Gambia.
(d) Explain how the government has reacted to the seasonal and spatial concentration of tourism in The Gambia.

Conclusion

The case studies show how several African governments have consistently supported tourism. In the five states discussed, tourism is now a significant sector of the national economy. Each state's industry is based on a different type of tourism: mass sunlust tourism in Tunisia, cultural tourism in Egypt, safari tourism in Kenya, trendsetting tourism in The Seychelles and winter sun tourism in The Gambia. These are a consequence of the original tourist appeal of each state and its accessibility from Europe, the main source of Africa's tourists. However, although mass sunlust tourism of the Tunisian variety is not likely to occur in the other chosen examples, a variety of sunlust tourism is prevalent in The Seychelles and The Gambia and is the most rapidly expanding type of tourism in Egypt and Kenya. Today, sun, sand and sea are Africa's outstanding attractions in the eyes of most tourists.

International tourism is believed by many economic planners to be a relatively easily created and reliable source of foreign exchange if suitable attractions exist. In the mid 1980s, in all the states considered, tourism was one of the top five export earners. In The Seychelles it totally dominates the export sector of the economy. The spread effects vary. The three larger states retain much of their tourist revenue and the hotels are supplied to some extent with locally produced food. Local industries provide some of the furnishings and craft workers make souvenirs. However, luxury items and wines and spirits expected by the tourists continue to be imported. In The Seychelles and The Gambia on the other hand, tourism has contributed to the rise of imports, including food. Tourism has helped to diversify economies and create a sector outside primary production. The small states had no option but to develop tourism as neither the copra of The Seychelles nor the groundnuts of The Gambia could ensure a secure future export income. Egypt, Kenya and Tunisia are large enough to consider the manufacturing option. All three have developed their manufacturing sector, mainly for the domestic market. Tourism has created jobs both directly and indirectly, and in the three larger states tourism has been used to develop areas away from the capital.

Selected use of statistics can easily support the case for international tourism. However, for a balanced assessment, the costs must also be considered.

Tourism competes with other sectors for scarce resources. Public money needed to build hotels and roads could have been used for agriculture, schools, health care, etc. Land prices in tourist areas have risen beyond the purchasing power of many local farmers. Seasonal demand for labour may cause neglect of agriculture. Tourism has contributed to general inflation, including that of food prices as in The Seychelles. In the arid states such as Egypt and Tunisia, hotels and tourist golf courses put pressure on the water supply.

It seems that tourism also increases spatial inequality. It benefits certain regions within a state. In Tunisia the coast has been favoured, in Egypt, the already congested middle Nile Valley. The rapid growth of tourism on the main island of Mahé in The Seychelles has contributed to the depopulation of some of the smaller islands. In The Gambia, tourism has enhanced the economic importance of Banjul and the adjacent Atlantic coast.

Tourists are by no means universally liked. By average African standards they are rich and they expect luxury and service in impoverished countries. Most have little interest in the host country's society and culture (beyond watching 'tribal dances' for evening entertainment at the hotel) and they can be very insensitive. They are also invariably white and come from the nations which, until recently, colonised Africa. In particular, orthodox Muslims see tourists as representatives of western decadence. Resentment of the tourist can range from sullen indifference to acts of violence, as have occurred recently in Egypt. The hostility of some groups within the states studied is at variance with the attitude of their governments. For the governments, the economic rewards justify the social costs. Only in The Seychelles has the government been sensitive to the envy, unfulfillable hopes and desires which international tourism may generate.

The economies of some African states have become so dependent on tourism that, even if their governments were responsive to the deep-rooted tensions it tends to create, they would find it difficult to foresake it. All five states have even greater need for foreign exchange than they had on independence. They all spend more on imports than they receive from exports and they need to pay back foreign debts (see Table 35). These countries find that they are enmeshed in a web of international obligations. Foreign exchange is required to fulfil these obligations.

This dependence has made these economies particularly vulnerable to events over which they have no control. Outside influences can easily disturb the tourist industry. African tourism has been developed largely for foreigners and is marketed by foreigners. Price increases, political instability, bad publicity and changing fashions can all influence a tourist's choice of destination. In the last ten years the number of tourist arrivals in each of these states has fluctuated from year to year as tourists respond to changing events. Capacity is not filled, predictions are not met, revenue is less than anticipated. Yet all the host states can do is to try and keep their prices competitive, maintain civil order, ensure high standards and persuade the international tourist companies to market their holidays with even more vigour. So the cost of tourism to African states has been increased pressure on scarce resources, greater spatial and social inequality, rising levels of tension and more dependence on foreign countries.

Mathieson and Wall (1982) observed that 'It is ironic that the destinations with the most to gain from tourism also appear the most vulnerable to its undesirable consequences'. Tourism provides foreign exchange, creates employment, diversifies the economy, assists regional development — all facets of economic development. Yet is it *real* development if inequality, social tensions and dependence are increased? It also appears that international tourism is the exploitation of Africa's resources primarily for the benefit of the people from the old colonial powers. The chosen destination may receive incidental benefits but these will grow or decline depending on the will of the sending countries. Tourism in Africa may be seen as a form of neocolonialism. This is to say that although the receiving countries are politically independent, their economic fate is largely dependent on decisions made by foreigners.

Added to this, tourism makes considerable demands on African states. The tourists expect the best a country can offer, including luxury and service. Most foreign tourists in Africa stay in hotels with private bathrooms and a swimming pool within the grounds. They prefer resorts containing several hotels and a variety of other tourist amenities. In these expensively produced resorts the tourists 'fun palaces' contrast starkly with the prevailing poverty. Yet without such resorts many of the tourists would not come. The dilemma is how to maximise economic gains and limit social costs. Many African governments consider the gains so great and the international financial obligations so pressing that they cannot do without tourism. With this in mind, ex-President Nyerere of Tanzania referred to tourism as a 'necessary evil'.

Two approaches might help to reduce the social costs. Firstly, the tourists could be isolated in specially built enclaves. They would then enjoy the African climate and beaches but have little contact with the people. Alternatively, only those tourists willing to stay in local guest houses and to eat national dishes and who wish to learn about the people, would be welcome. The first approach would be difficult to implement,

Table 35 Foreign trade deficit and debt, 1983

Country	Population	Trade deficit[1] ($ million)	Debt ($ million)	Debt/p.c. ($ US)	Tourism revenue ($ million)
Egypt	44,530,000	785	15,531	349	469
The Gambia	640,000	55	164	273	20
Kenya	1,878,000	174	2384	127	187
The Seychelles	64,000	27	42	700	33
Tunisia	6,890,000	561	3427	497	573

[1] This figure is the deficit on goods and services.

the second would lead to a considerable reduction in tourists. Both would be opposed by powerful groups who see no need for radical change.

Among these groups would be the present (1987) leadership of Tunisia, Kenya, Egypt and The Gambia. Tourism is partly a result of their 'open door' economic policy, emphasising foreign investment and exports. Tourism is an export industry and because it has grown far more rapidly than most other export industries, especially in the 1970s, it is seen as successful. The revenue from tourism has become indispensible in countries desperately short of foreign exchange. So, African governments continue to invest in the tourist industry, raising standards and trying to make it more competitive. African tourism has acquired its own momentum. The pleasure-seeking invaders have left their mark.

Assignments

1   Choose two Third World countries with differing government attitudes towards tourism and discuss how these have affected the development of the industry and of the economy as a whole.

Questions from A level examination papers

2   Examine the role of tourism in assisting regional economic development in any developing country. (Associated Examining Board, November 1983)
3   Assume that you have been commissioned to report on the tourist industry in any one of the case study areas. Write your report, dividing it into the following sections:
    (a) a description of the current state of the tourist industry including, (i) the main sources of visitors by country of origin; (ii) the location and characteristics of the areas and centres to which the tourists are attracted.
    (b) an outline of the prospects for the future development of tourism including, (i) the identification of tourist attractions (physical, cultural and scientific) which are currently under-developed; (ii) the infrastructure (*sic*) developments which would be necessary before their potential could be realised.
    (c) a discussion of the social and economic advantages and disadvantages which could result from the growth of the tourist industry. (Joint Matriculation Board, June 1983)
4   Account for the recent growth of leisure industries and suggest the spatial patterns likely to emerge at the national scale over the next few years. (Oxford and Cambridge 'S' level, July 1986)
5   For one area or more, examine the development of tourism and the environmental problems it creates. (London, June 1986)

References

Basdevant, D. (1986), *Egypt* (John Bartholomew and Times Books)

Blake, G. H. and Lawless, R. I. (1972), 'Algeria's tourist industry', *Geography*, vol. 57 (2)

Burkart, A. J. and Medlik, S. (1974), *Tourism, past, present and future* (Heinemann)

Cohen, E. (1974), 'Who is a tourist? A conceptual classification', *Sociological Review*, vol. 22

Economist Intelligence Unit (1978), Kenya, National Report no. 49, *International Tourism Quarterly*, vol. 8 (4)

(1980), Egypt, National Report no. 59, *International Tourism Quarterly* vol. 10 (1)

(1983), Tunisia National Report no. 83, *International Tourism Quarterly*, vol. 13 (2)

(1983), The Gambia, National Report no. 85, *International Tourism Quarterly*, vol. 13 (3)

(1985), The Seychelles, National Report no. 105, *International Tourism Quarterly*, vol. 15 (3)

(1986), Kenya, National Report no. 122, *International Tourism Report*, 1/4

(1987), Egypt, National Report no. 127, *International Tourism Report*, 2/1

Elkan, W. (1975), 'The relation between tourism and employment in Kenya and Tanzania', *Journal of Development Studies*, vol. 11

Farver, J. A. M. (1984), 'Tourism and employment in The Gambia', *Annals of Tourist Research*, vol. 11 (2)

Feifer, M. (1985), *Going places* (Macmillan)

Franda, M. (1982), *The Seychelles, unquiet islands* (Westview)

Gailey, H. (1964), *A history of The Gambia* (Routledge and Kegan Paul)

Gitau, J. M. (1984), 'Success and progress of tourism in Kenya', *The Tourist Review*

Hemingway, E. (1935), *Green hills of Africa* (Grafton)

Hopwood, D. (1985), *Egypt, politics and society, 1945–84* (Allen & Unwin)

Institute Espanol de Tourismo (1984), 'Spain and Mediterranean package holiday competition in 1983', *Tourist Management*, 5/2

Jackson, R. T. (1973), 'Problems of tourist development on the Kenyan coast', *Geography*, vol. 58 (1)

Jafari, J. (1973), *Role of tourism on socio-economic transformations of developing countries* (Cornell University, Ithaca, NY)

Jarrett, H. R. (1962), *Africa* (Macdonald and Evans)

de Kadt, E. (ed.) (1979), *Tourism, passport to development?* (World Bank, Oxford University Press)

Kahn, H. (1979), 'Leading futurologist traces next century of travel', *Trade Travel News*, 31/1

Kenya (1969), *5 year development plan (second), 1970–1974* (Ministry of Planning and National Development)

Kidron, M. and Segal, R. (1984), *The new state of the world atlas* (Pluto Press)

Lionnet, G. (1972), *The Seychelles* (David and Charles)

Lundberg, D. E. (1980), *The tourist business*, 4th ed. (Cahners Boston, USA)

Malcomson, S. (1984), 'Selling the exotic', *New Internationalist*

Martin, F. (1984), 'Tourism fuels Egypt's economy', *Hotels and Restaurants International*, vol. 18 (8)

Mathieson, A. R. and Wall, G. A. (1982), *Tourism, economic, physical and social impact* (Longman)

Mitchell, F. (1970), 'The value of tourism in East Africa', *East African Economic Review*, vol. 2

Murphy, P. E. (1985), *Tourism, a community approach* (Methuen)

Naylor, K. (1986), *Guide to West Africa* (Michael Haag)

O'Grady, R. (1981), *Third World stopover: the tourism debate* (World Council of Churches)

Pearce, D. (1981), *Tourist development* (Longman) (1987), *Tourism today, a geographical analysis* (Longman)

Peters, M. (1969), *International tourism* (Hutchinson)

Pullan, R. A. (1983), 'Do national parks have a future in Africa?', *Leisure Studies*, vol. 2 (1)

Rake, A. (ed.) (1986), *Travellers' guide to West Africa*, (I.C. Magazines)

Rice, B. (1968), *Enter Gambia, the birth of an improbable nation* (Angus and Robertson)

Senegalo-Gambia permanent secretariat, *The Gambia, the land and people*, Senegalo-Gambia tourist guide (Les Nouvelles Editions Africaines)

Sharp, J. (1981), 'The Port el Kantaoui tourist complex and regional consequences' in Harris, R. and Lawless, D. (eds.) *Field studies in Tunisia* (University of Durham)

Smith, D. M. (1979), *Where the grass is greener, living in an unequal world* (Penguin)

Swinglehurst, E. (1982), *Cook's tours; the story of popular travel* (Blandford Press)

Tarbush, S. (1985), 'Egypt's untapped tourist potential', *Middle East*, vol. 125

The Seychelles (1983), *National development plan, 1984–88* (Statistical Division)

Thuens, H. L. (1976), 'Notes on the Economics of International Tourism in Developing Countries', *Tourist Review*, vol. 31 (3)

Tunisia (1982), *Sixth economic and social plan, 1982–86* (Ministere de l'economique nationale)

Turing, P. (1982), *Traveller's Guide to Egypt* (Geographia)

Turner, L. and Ash, J. (1975), *The golden hordes, international tourism and pleasure periphery* (Constable)

Young, G. (1973), *Tourism, blessing or blight?* (Penguin)

Index